Beyond the Breaking of the Stone

A Collection of Poems

Paul Georgiou

Published by Panarc International 2019

Copyright © Paul Georgiou, 2019

First Edition

The author asserts the moral right under the Copyright, Designs and Patents Act 1988 to be identified as the author of this work.

All rights reserved. No part of this publication may be reproduced, stored in a retrieval system or transmitted, in any form or by any means without the prior consent of the author, nor be otherwise circulated in any form of binding or cover other than that in which it is published and without a similar condition being imposed on the subsequent purchaser.

www.panarcpublishing.com

Panarc International Ltd
www.panarc.com

Illustrations: Daria Mitchell

978-0-9956801-7-3 (Print)
978-0-9956801-8-0 (Epub)
978-0-9956801-9-7 (Kindle)

For my wife, my son and my daughter

Contents

Introduction   ix

Love
In the beginning   3
A mystery   4
Time drift in candlelight   5
A just equality   7
Not moist, red lips   9
Never a word so much abused as love   10
Two thousand weeks hence   12
Words   14
The edge of the sky   15
Antic possibilities   17
No way of telling   19
Beyond the breaking of the stone   21
My version of Sappho's prayer to Aphrodite   22

Anger, Madness & Despair
Over the green fields   27
India   29
The News on TV   31
Poor old dear   33
Love is made   35
Betrayal   36
The eyes of mole   37
The wild fragment man   38
The sea mew   39
Last brick in the wall   40
No chance   41

Conflict & War

The enemy within	45
The battle is over	49

Danger & Fear

The hunter's moon	53
Secrets of a dark and impious kind	54
The slayer and the slain	56
Pride	57
Beneath the roots of giant trees	58

God

I know God	61
It is possible	62
To crucify a man	64
Disjunction	68
Why	70
Prayer to the Lord	72
Given time	73
So there you are	76
This is how God is made	79
Rust	81
From a Christian to his Islamist brother	84
I would that God	88

Hope

This then I swear	91
This ancient earth of ours is fair	93
Voice of life	94
After all	96
Love distilled	98

Life

Life's elements	101
One should never leave one's home	102
What might I do!	104
Venus arose	105
Even a busy urban man	106
The measurements of man	107
This and that	108
Uncertainty	110
The twig	112
Sleep	113
A kind deceit	114
Dry leaves, wizened, lifeless	115
Walls	117
Rambling	118
A father's song	121
Sum ergo sum	123
The sentence of life	126
Cause, effect, time and broken rhymes	128
The unexamined life	130
We smuggled love into the world	131
The first mistake	134

Occasional Poems

Essay on man and woman	139
A father's thoughts	144

Stories

Ibn Saud	149
The tortoise and the hare	152

Lyrics

There's a way	159
Square One – theme song	160
Day of days	161

Stuff & Nonsense

Song of the Pongid	165
The Pongid lament	166
Paean to Pong	167
On the discovery of the Hog's Bison	169
Normandy	170
Let's pretend	171
There was a man	172
The undoing of the rapper	174
Negation	176
Whales never fail	177
A parable of war	179
Ringwood wood	180
Tricky	180
An Amorusc expedition	181
Evolution	181
Index of First lines	183

Introduction

I have had two obsessions in my life: words and ideas.

I love words for many reasons. First of all, mastering them is an unending challenge. They are the most precise and subtle means of communication at our disposal but, given half a chance, they can become tricky and unruly. When I am writing an analytical piece, I sometimes think that persuading words to do exactly what I want is not dissimilar to herding cats. At other times, when writing poetry, I revel in exploiting their many layers of meaning, their rich connotations, their easy ambiguity and, above all, their sonic characteristics which give us rhythm and rhyme, alliteration and assonance.

As for ideas, they live in an infinite world that transcends the petty constrains of time and space. We have one body and a few, fairly limited senses. We have one life and, however adventurous we may be, we are subject to temporal and spatial constraints. But there is a world where there are no limits, the world of creativity and imagination.

That's why I write. Man is a meaning-seeking creature. We have an undeniable need to ask how and why. We look for answers to 'how?' in science and mathematics. For answers to 'why?' questions, we have to search in our experience of life and to explore the world of ideas, those of others and our own.

That's when, for me, words and ideas, suitably arranged, come together in a happy confluence of sound and meaning, signifying something worthwhile.

The poems in this book are written in various forms and styles. Some rhyme; some don't. The meaning of some is perfectly straightforward; others are multi-layered. I'm hoping everyone will find at least one or two poems that, for them, come close to meeting one of poetry's objectives, of conveying "what oft was thought, but ne'er so well expressed". I also hope that some readers will be interested in poems that explore ideas that are less commonly thought.

Some of the poems deal with contentious issues; some contain sexually explicit lines and provocative thoughts. If I offend anyone, I apologise. But everyone should have the right to say what they think, just as everyone has the right to disagree or criticise.

Enough! Enjoy!

Paul Georgiou
June, 2018

LOVE

In the beginning

In the beginning
    a man a woman found
    beneath the tree of life
and they made love
and saw that it was good,
being of one mind.

Then one of them
    but which we do not know
    though each the other blamed
made a mistake,
finding fault but was unsure,
being in two minds.

The other, or perhaps the same,
    for as time passes it is difficult
    to know such things,
made fun of love
which, though both understood,
neither forgave.

So they walked alone, each other forsaking
while the years fell like leaves on the grave of their aching.
And their story is ended – though some men say
that once each year they make their way
to a distant half-forgotten night
and make love on the earth for each other's delight.

And the leaves are stirred, though no winds blow,
beneath the tree of long ago.

A mystery

For me you weave a mystery
with countless secrets up your sleeve
and distant journeys in your eyes:
and should I talk to you for years
involved with laughter, words and tears,
and should I lie between your thighs
and contemplate your smiles and sighs,
there still would be a mystery
of what it is you want from me.

The Sphynx, reclining on the sand,
had visitors from every land:
when Pilate asked "Pray, what is truth?"
his laughter cracked the temple roof.
There's ample proof in history
that we all love a mystery.
So I shall keep a secret too
of what it is I want from you.

Time drift in candlelight

Time drift
in candle-light
such a game
leap-flame
insight
out of sight
out of mind
out of play
end game.

Bright curve
celebrate
warm touch
illuminate
candle-light
time drift
insight.

Time drift
in eye light
sun twist
of end night
from here
so near
time drift
age scar.

Pain in limb
pain of life
counter strife
insane
out-witted
half-witted
in witted
in time.

No sense
no point
out of joint
no defence –
yet such a sight
such a gift
candle-light
time drift.

A just equality

If I to you
were, am, untrue,
then either I must speak the truth
or lie;
and either you are hurt or not
or neither.

And if you do not feel,
although you know,
my infidelity
and, as I with another lie,
so you,
and tell the truth
to him or me
and he or I am hurt
or not;
then let us grant
that you and I are humankind
(and she and he)
and in a very sad-go-round
press hard the wine
and crush the juice
(or so it seems)
out of my, your (and his, her) dreams:
and this for independence sake,
or fear
that those who one another take
must give or break.
Yet let us both agree
that you and I decide
or not
that such a fear is justified.

"One thing is sure;"
she smilingly replied
"In 'either or'
resides a just equality,
and thus you lose the argument,
or so it seems,
while I have nothing lost
except your dreams."

Not moist, red lips

Not moist red lips, nor limpid eyes,
nor subtle undulating flesh,
nor breasts of cream, pink nipples fresh,
nor soft recidivistic thighs,
nor all the strange spasmodic bliss
that lurks within that orifice
where scent of myrrh, breath of the sea,
cause lonely cries of ecstasy

can bind as tightly as a smile,
as firmly as a gentle word.
Exchange excludes, demands defile;
indifference leaves love undeterred.
Those eyes ensnare that recognise
 love is a gift and not a prize.

Never a word so much abused as love

Never a word so much abused as love.
"I am afraid, so stay and share my fear"
a common usage it is clear,
which can be heard in whispers everywhere.

Another meaning, and perhaps
the commonest, is "I give up my dreams,
forget my bold ambition and my hopes,
and, in despair, accept what seems
not best but tolerable."

Another sense,
and these are not exclusive definitions
of the word, is "You have what I want,
yes, you are what I need; and hence
to satisfy the want and need in me,
you, I will take." Strange as it may seem to be
this taking is called love.

There is, of course, another way that love
is meant; rarer in use, in practice rarer still.
Its core is giving and its heart is this;
"I feel myself in you; therefore I will
share and dissolve your fears; all that you dream
with you I wish to build, for in such building
we will find
whatever is the best in you and me
and all mankind.
My sole desire shall be
not what I want or need but how I may
enrich for you the progress of each day."

Love

The rabble of events and life's exigencies
conspire against love of this kind.
But it may be, and who can say,
if you and I are of a mind
and have the will to bind and stay,
together we may find a way.

Two thousand weeks hence

Two thousand weeks hence
and the present a far distant half-forgotten play in which
aliens affected to be us,
will we remember with remorse
or pity
or with the pleasure
of those whom age has made invulnerable
our love?

Will you, the mother of a mother,
think of me one evening
when your memory has
nothing
better to do,
and smile?
And will you while away
a moment of old age
in idle play
with possibilities?

I see you now
looking on
while younger organisms
create and nurture and outgrow
all the ancient errors of our ways:
but for us (as for them)
our own mistakes (and theirs)
will have a majesty
that gives the lie to truth.

Love

We will grow old
but that of me I gave to you,
that which you gave to me,
is ours to love and honour
for as long as we so wish
even, through the lovers
with whom we spend our nights,
through the days of success and failure,
through the filling of the vacant future
even, should we so wish it,
till two thousand weeks hence.

Words

How many times have you and I
discussed the power of words to tell
the deepest feelings that we have,
the drives that come from heart or will?

And I have said that words will do
for, failing words, what other way
can tell those things which move us most?
Silence absorbs what we would say.

But now I see that you are right
for I have thoughts which words betray.
I love you more than words can tell
and I shall love you more each day.

And, in the end, when time is done,
and you and I must stand alone,
if there is silence, then know this,
which I now seal with touch and kiss:
you are the woman of my life,
my friend, my mistress and my wife;
in good or bad times to the end
I am your husband, lover, friend.

The edge of the sky

Tell me a story of ancient times
and tell me the truth:
we, who are young, are old enough
to listen to both.
In and out of my empty skull
flutters the call of a gull.

    Did we not talk
    beneath a Thracian sky
    when Alexander ruled in Macedon
    and look at stars
    which here tonight
    we still may look upon?

    Was it in Samarkand
    that many years ago
    we bathed our bodies
    in the waters of the Zerafshan
    where horses from the steppes drank deep and long?

    Did we not meet again
    beneath a tree along the Appian Way
    where Spartacus was crucified
    and smile to think how small
    the world was then?
    I saw your face again in Syracuse
    when I was dragged from Athens in defeat.

    The night that Scipio came
    with half of Rome,
    did I not lie with you
    in Carthage
    long ago?

Each time we crossed each others path
we both asked why
though ages passed.

Do you remember how
when once we met
beside an endless, sunswept shore
a great sea-eagle left the land
and we pursued it, you and I,
uplifted, outstretched by its confident cry,
till the wings of the bird
touched the edge of the sky?

Antic possibilities

They passed the day
in mental play
with antic possibilities;
and she would turn
all upside down
and smiling watch
her lover frown,
until her lover, brave with fear,
persuaded all to disappear.

And so they dallied, all day long
singing a strange conceptual song
until the night when bodies rise
to play between each other's thighs.
One night while lying close entwined
a crooked thought sprang from his mind
and clutching words to hide its shame
(for thoughts disrupt the body's game)
enquired what gift her love could bring
to make him of her comfort sing.

She started, sighed,
and then replied,
"I will love you
till such time
as I choose to cease to love;
and I shall honour you,
through all my days,
– or till the memory of you fades –
as you deserve;

I shall obey
throughout our love
my wishes, my desires, myself.
Such is my love
and honesty the gift I bring
to make you of my comfort sing."

HE
"Is this the gift you offer me
when we are lying close entwined?"

SHE
"It is a noble gift I give,
the naked love of womankind."

HE
"But such a thing is common-place
and may be found in any face."

SHE
"But is not honesty a thing
to make you of my comfort sing?"

HE
"There's comfort in my love for you
whether my love is false or true.
Your honesty describes a state
too common-place to contemplate.
The truth you tell creates a thing
too common-place to sing;
and that philosophy is wrong
which cannot find its place in song."

No way of telling

There is no way of telling when,
in laughter, argument, or tears,
in long debate of other loves,
in living through the learning years;

there is no way of telling when,
from pictures catching olden days,
when all seemed simpler far than now
and simpler was in many ways;

there is no way of telling when,
despite the different roads we walked
with others closer to us both
with whom we lived and loved and talked;

there is no way of telling when
your hopes and fears became for me
more than a game of hide and seek,
became for me reality.

We do not live in ancient times
when heroes rescued maidens fair:
the enemies that stalk our land
are lies, deceit and lack of care;
they have no substance and no form,
no sword can kill, no shield defend;
their shadow threatens all of us
and may destroy us in the end.

But this I say in honesty –
I know you well and yet I say –
I find a quality in you
a gentle, rare and precious thing
as bright as any day.

And this I promise, this I swear,
though time and space may us divide,
through all the joy and pain we meet,
in battles won or in defeat,
I shall be at your side.

Beyond the breaking of the stone

Our love, my love,
is young and old;
strong-limbed and lithely bold
but lined and underlined
by many lives of long ago
whose names, though some were cut in stone,
survived alone within the mind.

In youth, my love, our bodies touch
and join;
naked we wrestle tenderly
and shudder at the pleasure that we find;
we give and take
until, my love, with love we break,
though still in loose delight entwined.

But in its age, our love, my love
was old when you and I alone,
surveyed with other eyes the Nile
and seeing Khufu build his pyramid
– the endless laying on of stone on stone –
looked at each other openly,
a wise awareness in the smile we gave
that, in a thousand lives of love,
our love, my love, would long outlive
the grandeur of the Pharaoh's grave.

From then till now, in youth and age,
throughout the thousand lives we've known,
a thousand lovers, hand in hand,
declare our love, their love, survives;
at every time, in every land,
beyond the flesh, beyond the bone,
beyond the breaking of the stone.

My version of Sappho's prayer to Aphrodite

Listen to me, lovely, lissom-limbed daughter of Zeus,
Aphrodite, immortal meddler with mere mortal minds.
Show mercy to me; mistress, make my breaking heart whole.
You know without doubt what I crave for and why.

I have a kindness to ask. I know you can hear me,
'though mountains and seas are between us, my saviour.
Quit the home of your father and come to me quickly,
as you, Aphrodite, have done so before.

Guide your chariot of old gold, yoking the winged ones,
avian masters of air, through azure skies soaring,
deeply despising the dull, leaden doldrums of earth
in their fabulous, effortless flying so high.

You come to me. I lay myself down for your beauty,
bemused by the life that glows and gleams from your body.
See I suffer so sorely. You must soften my pain,
unendurable pain, please help me once more.

You ask whom I crave for, yes, whose cruelty cuts me;
and you ask whom I ask you to teach how to love me.
My aching desire consumes me, the whole world must know;
there is, for me, but one – all others above.

> "I am here. I will help you, Sappho, sister in love,
> The young girl who rejects will, ere long, long to touch you.
> The gifts she dares to send back, soon shall she send to you,
> yes, whether or not it is what she may wish."

Love

Great Aphrodite, divine, devious, beautiful,
you assume all my aching and assuage it with love.
We are bound tight together in deep understanding;
you are my fair friend – and my lover, my love.

Anger, Madness & Despair

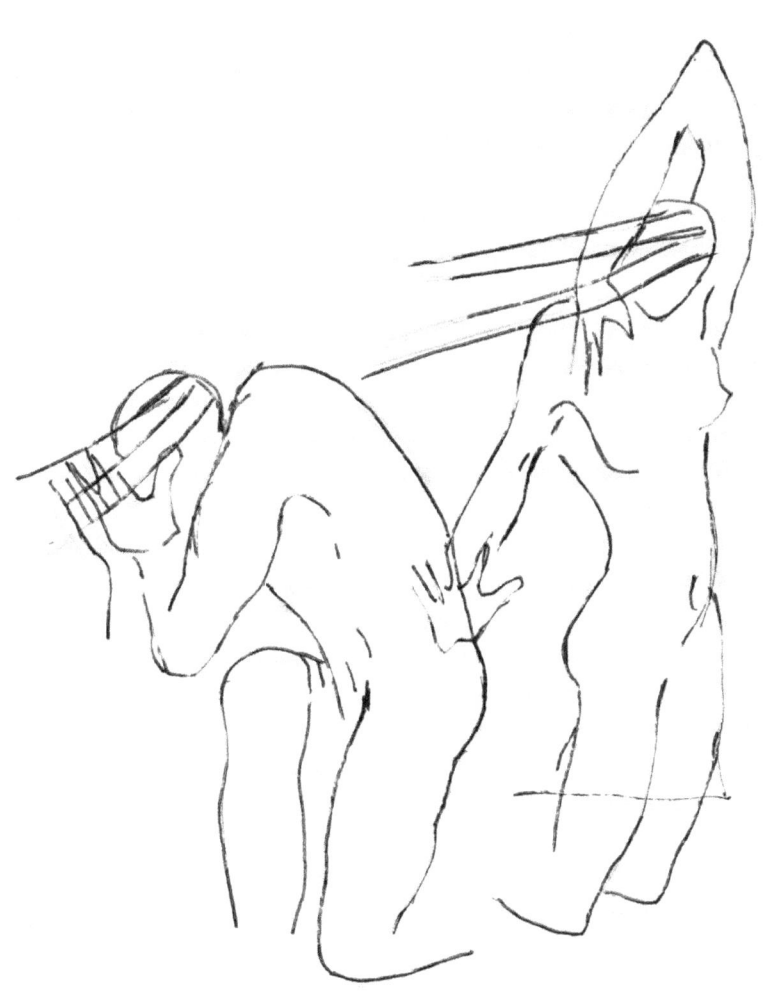

Over the green fields

Potatoes, peas, pornography,
honour, truth, orthography,
kisses, crosses, crucifixion,
judgement-passing from conviction;
hold the hand that holds the pen,
fuller, faster, tell me when:
tend the burn but burn the children,
virgin blood in strumpet cauldron;
paint the walls with pretty pictures,
"Buy" or "Die," enticements, strictures.
Tear the eye from every socket,
break the chain and sprain the sprocket.

Over the green fields far away
voyeurs give a seedy cough,
while old lovers and their lasses
regularly have it off.

Up and down and round and round
empty words reverberate!
Hear the barker's call resound –
"Roll up, roll on,
it's not too late."
One more show before we go;
buy your tickets, clap your hands,
slap your thighs and feel your glands.
You've seen freaks that fornicate,
seen the maggot on the plate.
It's the last laugh so laugh loudly,
here's a pageant painted proudly;
see the vagrants at the gate,
see the martyrs lie in state,
see the cretin contemplating,
see the eunuch masturbating.

Over the green fields far away
seven sages sit and wait,
While beneath their snow-white mantles
seven bladders urinate.

Let us burn the ancient people
buried now in institutions;
we'd be rich if we could save in-
surance bloody contributions.
I am worth what I can earn,
I deserve what I inherit;
talk a little less of beggars
and a little more of merit.
Potatoes, peas, pornography,
fat and poor, geography,
cash and castles, pox and palaces,
dripping down from drooping phalluses;
rich is rich and thin is thin,
all must fight and all shall win
honesty the only sin …
Over the green fields far away
starving children wonder why,
while their strange, despotic fingers
mutilate a bloated fly.

India

At the end of yesterday,
after dark had dropped
from the bedside lamp
into the corners of my eyes,
I lay in my hot body
in your bed,
aware and yet untouched,
and listened, sweating,
to the chaukeedaars of Delhi
warbling to each other
through the night.

O the whistle and drum,
the ubiquitous hum,
and the evil mosquito's most intimate whine;
ribald colours that rush
from a lunatic brush
to disport in a world of delinquent design.

The middle night bustles
with crowds of images;
men walking arm in arm
past beggars with no hands
or legs;
girls of great beauty
sail along,
their bodies brown
and smooth in saris,
breezes of jasmine
across the acrid smell
of open sewers,
aware and yet untouched.

O the whistle and drum,
the ubiquitous hum,
and the evil mosquito's most intimate whine;
ribald colours that rush
from a lunatic brush
to disport in a world of delinquent design.

Behold the bold hermaphrodite –
tall, breasted, flashing eyed and grossly coy;
the policeman beating wildly at a boy
whose limbs are thinner than the stick that beats;
the dog which has a marble for one eye;
observe the characters of famine and of pain
that posture on the busy city streets,
aware and yet untouched;
unmoved by chaukeedaars upon their nightly rounds;
places of silence, refugees from life,
the darkest colours and smallest sounds.

Before dawn,
we lie by each other.
The insect that drinks blood
follows the dark
and stings behind the eye.

O the whistle and drum,
the ubiquitous hum,
and the evil mosquito's most intimate whine;
ribald colours that rush
from a lunatic brush
to disport in a world of delinquent design.

The News on TV

I was seated one day
with my mind far away
and my eyes mesmerised by the box I despised
when my sanity stumbled
recovered then crumbled;
the thing I most cherished had finally perished
as I sat in the den
at one minute to ten
on the night that my brain succumbed to the strain.

There I was, as I said,
having gone off my head,
defeated I clung to the arms of my chair,
when the telly stood up
and proffered a cup
of laxative mixed with Heineken beer.
As I drank and then farted
the 'News at Ten' started.
Well what could I do but see what was new?

'Absurd,' you declare,
'If your mind had gone spare
then surely you'd never, your mind gone forever,
remain in your chair
and hark to with care,
much less to wish to see, the News on TV?'
You forget, my dear friend,
I was ill at each end,
insane and half-pissed, and my bowels in a twist.
So I stayed where I was
quite simply because
the news on the box should never be missed.

THE NEWS AT TEN
'The Trades Unions make an offer, the employers have rejected.
The Prime Minister is lonely; body odour is suspected.
Hypothermia is harnessed to control the population
and the police are now enforcing the ban on copulation
(though confusion has arisen in the Parliamentary Lobbies
since the law was to discourage sex between consenting Bobbies).
A call girl of most high renown resigns from her profession
for lying with a Minister throughout an all-night session
"If bread's becoming pricey," a quote from the Queen Mother,
"instead of knocking monarchy, why don't they eat each other?"
A late night flash – two comets enter orbit around Venus,'
whereat the newscaster unzipped and showed his balls and penis.
END OF NEWS

At this I decided
(the beer had subsided
and the laxative trouble had burst in a bubble)
that a man who's insane
must do more than complain.
I prepared to destroy once
for all this annoyance.
With calm, controlled manner
I picked up a spanner,
moved away from my chair,
from the very spot where
my once healthy mind
had slowly declined
and I shattered the screen where the News had just been.

I had won. It was dead.
Then from nowhere it said;
"Please do not forget to switch off your head."

Poor old dear

Poor old dear
with bleary eyes,
clutching your empty carrier bag.
Come here.

No lies.

Are you mother, spinster
or some other?

Are you one
who lost a son?
Then you are
forever
grieving mother.

Were you married
but outlived
the one you wed?
Then you are widow.

Or did your marriage fail?
Some would say
marriages don't fail.
People fail.
Are you failure,
or worse,
victim?

Or were you never married?
Then you are old maid.

I ask you now.
What are you now?

Are you now a burden?

Or are you quite alone –
a breath of pity
that slips between the words
that stumble round you?

Love is made

Love is made,
desires persist,
in the movement of a wrist.

Hope, by nature, will transcend
disappointment in the end.

For a moment self-hood dies
in the branches of the thighs.

Do not forget the bedrock, friend;
paper, women; pencil, men:
doodling in each other's laps;
a semi-paradox perhaps,
but such a thought is seminal.

Reality lies
upon my word,
your word,
the word;
known yet seldom spoken
and still less seldom heard.
Shouted down by the present tense
where grunts can masquerade as sense.

Never forget the bedrock, friend,
on which the word takes precedence
not hope, not love
which are but words
that we can only half defend
if we forget
the word is all –
beginning, middle,
and the end.

Betrayal

I'm afraid
I have forgotten
what it was
that I betrayed;
but the soul
my ways have stolen
was already
half decayed.

> I could tell another story
> of the power and the glory,
> of the glory that departed,
> of the power that has stayed.

But I wish I could remember
on that evening last December
how we laughed and how we played,
what we said and how I prayed
that the thing I have forgotten
shouldn't by me be betrayed.

The eyes of mole

I'm losing myself within my head,
a place of enormous hollowness,
like a flea embalmed in a double-bed
or a man adrift inside his head.

Heaven is a salad in all its gay apparel
and I am the worm creating holes
which thrives in the context of salad bowls
while rucking the lawn like a little blind mole.
There's crap in every barrel.

The head in which I'm lost is mine;
I make the bed where I recline:
And I prepare the salad which I in time defile;
the bottom of my empty glass reflects a sober smile.
I peer beyond bed, bowl and hole,
how small so-e'er the eyes of mole.

The wild fragment man

"Love," and she clung to me;
"Yes," but I struggled free –
too many images hang in my mind.
Time is what I can see,
change stands immutably
hacking away at my hopes from behind.
Pictures and patterns fade,
structures that I have made
break into pieces that I cannot find.

"Now," let the moment be.
Honour such bravery.
Fear is a skull that is deaf, dumb and blind.
Words that I contemplate,
meaning I fabricate
fit at my will to the form of my plan.
Battered and desolate,
doubtful I hesitate;
where is the strength to insist that I can?

"Here," and she lay with me,
"Thus," and she played with me.
    "Laughter shall burst from the wild fragment man."

The sea mew

You are as empty as the sea
as hollow as the sky to me,
as lifeless as the grey-green land
on which the trees in coffins stand.
You are a ferret and a mole
which burrows deep into my soul,
but all you find is a little hole
where I another thing have planned.
You are a child that works in sand
where dreams dissolve and children sigh,
where a young girl sobs at the muted cry
of a sea mew lost in a hollow sky.

Last brick in the wall

Too many choices,
bickering voices,
nagging at me to make a decision.
Too much to understand,
none of it clear or planned;
out of my ears spout hoots of derision.

Not quite sure why or how,
only two choices now –
whittled it down to a straight 'either or'.
Whichever I choose
I seem certain to lose.
The noise in my head is now worse than before.

No choice at all,
last brick in the wall;
panic as I am locked into my head.
None to be heard or seen.
Nothing to choose between.
No choice at all. No more to be said.

No chance

So that's the way it is, my God, no chance
to rectify the past, to make amends;
on, ever on, allowed no backward glance,
no means to justify whatever ends:
each eager 'now' no sooner here than gone,
ensnared within the present's fleeting frame.
What's done always irrevocably done;
a baffled player in a cryptic game.

Despite the darkness, of your life make light;
there's little choice in any path you choose.
Be confident – each battle that you fight
is but a skirmish in a war you'll lose;
remember this, when life begins to fade,
you'll find yourself upon the bed you made.

Conflict & War

The enemy within

Stand on the castle parapet with me;
look down towards the deep, black velvet plain
which skirts the hill on which this castle stands,
look out into the darkness of the land,
peer through the dampness of the drizzling rain,
until with me you see the things I see.

See how, with guttering, uncertain light,
the distant fires of the enemy camps
prick pinholes in the fabric of the night.
Now hear the distant, ribald laughter of their soldiers
making merry, each comrade full of hazy, vacuous cheer,
drowning the dreadful thoughts of killing and of death
in blood-red wine and thick, warm, frothing beer.

Tomorrow they will come, as they have come before,
with a cacophony of warlike calls,
and they will batter at these mighty walls
like moths attracted to a flickering flame.
At hint of dawn, while good men lie asleep,
they will attempt to scale the eastern ramparts;
hurling huge boulders at the crenelated castle keep;
in an unending, pitiless and pointless game.

We will, as we have done so many times before,
dislodge them from their handholds on the stone,
pour boiling oil on their shaven heads,
set fire to their catapults with molten lead,
and shower them with arrows for their trouble,
until they shamble back, groaning in disarray,
leaving their dead and dying amongst the rain-wet rubble,
their faith in winning waning as light drains from the day.

> "Another waste of time. There is no point.
> A hundred men lie dead or wounded and our enemies
> look down upon us from their walls in disbelief.
> It is a crime. Our leaders count our dead in scores
> but are as careless of our lives, it's fair to say,
> as we are careless of our meagre pay
> when in the gaudy company of whores."

We fear these crazed marauders of the plain
and spend our time and energy, our wealth and our resources,
in building castles such as these, high up on hills
or mountain tops, with walls as massy as the hills themselves
to keep these killers out, to keep out those who kill,
who take delight is spreading terror and in causing pain.

> "I'm not a gambling man but I will stake my pay this month
> we lose more men tomorrow than we did today.
> It's tempting fate but I'd like you to take
> a wager I am not amongst the ones to die.
> Don't laugh my friend, it's not a joke.
> If I survive, I'll take some consolation from the winning of the bet.
> Should I be wrong, it won't hurt me to pay,
> and, if it turns out I am broke,
> then I shall die forever in your debt."

So let them come, these fritterers of lives,
gorged on the food and drink of honest men
whom they have butchered with their knives
to sate their hunger and their thirst for blood.
Let it be understood. They shall not scale these walls;
they'll not prevail, we will not fail this test; we will not fail.

> "If we could only force the gates or, with the trebuchet,
> annihilate their walls. If we could, while they sleep,
> creep under the black blanket of the night,
> slip past the lazy and complacent guards
> and reach and take the keep,
> then those who laugh at us would learn to weep."

For many years they struggled, besiegers and besieged,
The castle dwellers and the warriors of the plain,
Ten thousand died each year but still the castle stood
and every spring the feckless, futile siege began again.

There was no way the castle could be stormed.
The walls could not be broken, nor be scaled;
marauder leaders aged, grew tired and died
and new ones came with new plans newly formed,
and tactics they claimed heretofore untried.
But, well aware that all before had failed,
the soldiers knew for sure their leaders lied
when promising that they could turn the tide.

And yet the castle fell.

How it began is still unknown:
a word of disillusion or a frown,
a slight perceived, though not perhaps intended,
a privilege withdrawn or just suspended;
inadequate reward for service rendered.
Up to this day no-one can say
what drove the traitor to betray.
The only certainty is this;
no reason he could give could justify
why all within the castle had to die.

Throughout the years of siege and battles fought
the castle-dwellers never for one moment thought
the enemy that they had most to fear
was sharing with them draughts of castle beer
and feasting with them in the banquet hall,
on their side of the massy castle wall.

Yet that is how the mighty castle fell,
not broken by marauders from the plain
but foiled by an enemy within.
One storm black night of blinding rain
this creature shrieked in silent pain,
and, without hope of any gain
as far as anyone can tell,
with disregard none can explain,
unlocked the creaking gates of hell
and watched the slaughter of his kin begin.

The battle is over

I am weary,
the battle is over:
We have fought
and not lost
and not won.

Only ruins remain
to bear witness
to the tyrannous
things we have
done.

Our divisions disperse
through the rubble,
raising dust
that obscures
the sun,

While we look on
the days we have
wasted
on a quarrel remembered
by none.

Friend and foe,
let us go
to the fireside
where tales and lies
are spun,
and recall
all the glories of battle,
how we fought –
and how each of us
won.

Danger & Fear

The hunter's moon

The hunter's moon is high tonight
above the cold, fragmented ground.
Out of the stones and earth and trees
the colours bleed.
Beware the hunter's footfall
and the shadow of his hound.

Silent are the forests
where the snake and lizard lie,
and the ancient soil where man once slept
is silent too.
No cry of joy or pain is heard
beneath the deep, black sky.

Where the remnants of the cities rise
above neglected graves of State,
the blind eyes of the houses stare
but throw no light
upon the dark arena
where the traveller must wait.

The last child has walked this land,
forest and city are still;
only snake and lizard eyes
shall, in cold blood,
be witness to
the moment of the kill.

The hunter's moon is high tonight
above the cold, fragmented ground.
Out of the stones and earth and trees
the colours bleed.
Beware the hunter's footfall
and the shadow of his hound.

Secrets of a dark and impious kind

In the silent times of dreaming
when our daytime eyes are blind,
in some crevice of the body,
in some corner of the mind,
we may catch a glimpse of secrets
of a dark and impious kind.

* * *

Shadows flit across the landscape
into hollows of despair;
something lies in wait for victuals
in the blackness of its lair,
while a yellow mist sits heavy
on the dank and fetid air;

The sun at noon bleeds in the sky,
a dull and leaden red;
the thing that preyed on others
shall not again be fed.
Now nothing moves or breathes or lives;
the land itself is dead.

* * *

There is an ancient prophecy
that, when the earth was slain,
a wind arose from nowhere
over mountain, valley, plain,
and, through the hope the wind brought, fell
the solace of the rain.

It soothed the acrid soil
and streams began to flow;
in time, it reached the fissures
in the silent world below
and there, by chance, it found a seed;
the seed began to grow.

The mandrake seed, for such it was,
yearned upward through the earth;
it struggled through the mud and rock,
unmindful of its worth
or that the stricken planet was
reliant on its birth.

Too late it reached the surface.
Too late it touched the day.
A savage wind had risen
in an angry sky of grey.
There was a shriek that no-one heard,
The plant was swept away.

   * * *

And that is how the story ends
when every eye is blind;
no crevice in the body and
no corner of the mind:
at last, no more of secrets
of a dark and impious kind.

The slayer and the slain

The knife, high-poised above the stone,
the crowd, the priest, the tribal dream,
the sun in silence, then the scream,
a roar, a prayer, a mother's groan.

A wooden cross against the sky,
the spear upheld; at last the doubt:
the thunderclap, the sudden shout,
a soldier's laugh, a mother's cry.

The legs drawn back, the flesh is torn,
the head appears between the thighs;
the baby shrieks, the mother sighs,
the slayer and the slain is born.

Pride

Lethargic lions lurk along our motorways,
hedge-hid in tundric verges, silent, alert and still:
reviewing with cold, calmly calculating eyes
which of the passing thousands to mark out for the kill.

The endless, thoughtless herd of wildebeest rolls on,
aware but powerless to avoid the sly attack;
bemused by numbers and by more than generous odds,
only the wisest of the herd remember to look back.

The lions make their move, weaving towards their prey;
they speed and swerve and, merciless, pull down their prize.
The flowing herd moves past, a tad more slowly now,
to observe the kill with passive, semi-curious eyes.

The herd, less one, will not, must not and cannot stop;
it's not their lot in life even to wonder why.
They cluck and shrug and, if they think at all, they think:
"There – but for the random grace of God – go I."

"What is the point?" you ask. The herd is not disturbed.
They scarcely register one of their kind has died.
The lions lounge once more, their hunger fully sated –
no glory here to satisfy a lion's pride?

Beneath the roots of giant trees

There is a world the depth of which I am afraid,
where truth lies huddled in a dream
and threatens to invade my mind
with all the terrors of mankind –
worlds of forests, shuffling leaves,
children playing endlessly,
murdered by such hands as these
beneath the roots of giant trees.

God

I know God

I know God, a dirty old man,
used to write words on various walls;
mother – "I can't but I must understand,"
father – "Unknown but a man."

Totters around on bomb sites now
and plays hop-scotch with children
between piles of white rubble,
limping along after children run wild,
making slowly his way, as the sun gushes yellow,
his feet wrapped in old cloth
flod up the dust. The lines on his face
run rivers of dirt – strong lines, weak lines,
lines of long-living.

Mutters to passers-by; "I'm Lord of All,
or was once, of much."
Most cross the street
"Ought to be put away."
"Doesn't someone look after him?"
"Drunk!"

I don't mind, but I know him,
this God who wrote words on various walls;
mother – "I can't but I must understand."
father – "Unknown but a man."

It is possible

It is possible
that it was not the snake
which spoke
(for snakes can't speak)
but Adam, who,
in hours of boredom
had invented and perfected
the throwing of his voice
and wished to see
what happened
when Eve ate.

And it is possible
that Joseph was a cuckold
(for the Holy Ghost can't fuck)
and that Mary was unfaithful
and that Jesus was the cross
on which the love
that Joseph bore his wife
was nailed down
and rose again.

And it is possible
that with the death of God
we now concern ourselves so much
with here and now
and one another
in hope that we may find
an adequate support
for absolutes
like love and truth,
trust and fidelity.

And it is certain
that each of these
interpretations
is no more than possible –
for having lost the absolute
the only thing we need not doubt
is our uncertainty.

To crucify a man

O Lord, we, the management,
who hold it as our main responsibility
to rationalise wherever possible,
have now completed our examination
of the structure and the functions
of our company.

We trust the changes
that we deem expedient
will bring great benefits,
not only to the men
who have invested
in our enterprise,
but also to employees
who have sacrificed so much
to realise the targets we have set.

We are not unaware, O Lord,
of the long service
You have given to our company;
indeed, in jest, we often say
the company without You
would not be
the company at all.
But, be that as it may,
we know that You,
like us,
must wish to put
our enterprise before
considerations purely personal
and we are sure
that You will be
the first to grant
that time cannot stand still.

The introduction, Lord,
of modern management
has given us techniques
that You have proved
unwilling or unable to adopt;
the values You uphold,
while no doubt excellent
and pertinent in days of old,
are thought no longer
relevant to the attainment
of our goals.

Let it be said, in some respects,
they clearly hinder us
in the pursuit
of our objectives.
All this we know
is recognised by You;
in recent years
You have participated less
in all the many meetings
that expound the principles
whereby our enterprise shall grow.
Indeed Your absences
have been so regular that some
(the younger members of our staff)
have questioned whether You
exist or not.
Another joke of course
and one which, in a way,
pays homage to the dignity
with which You have
decided to
retire.

On such occasions, Lord, as this
no words can tell
the debt of gratitude
we owe.
Your loyalty to us
beyond the limit we, by right, might claim
burns as a beacon
throwing light on all.
We can but hope
that we who yet remain within this enterprise
will follow the example
You have shewn.

The staff will wish
to say goodbye
less formally.
But we, the management,
consider it our privilege
to offer you
a token of the high regard
in which You have been, are,
and always will be held.

Accept this presentation box,
a fine example of our marquetry,
a symbol of our company
constructed by the finest craftsmen
we employ;
within, to signify
the forceful purpose
of our enterprise,
a silver hammer
from our workshops
wrought with wondrous skill.

And finally, O Lord,
to represent
Board, Management and Staff
the mystery of Three in One
the lynchpins of our Five Year Plan,
we offer You with all our heart
three nails straight and strong enough
and, should you wish it, long enough
to crucify a man.

Disjunction

ME
Bones, beneath the skin of metaphor,
all pleasure now unmemoried,
long past the dark declivities of shame
when flesh has turned to dust,
I have to pick with you.

What, on earth or elsewhere, when,
in impish indolence or mean intent,
with, we surmise, complacent gesture,
you composed your grand design,
were you, divine one, thinking of?

It's not our praise which by tradition is,
of all that we might give,
the thing you prize most high
but, given our intolerable predicament,
forgiveness you should yearn.

You must have known, when you made 'when',
and 'now' and 'then', that time condemned
each living thing to an inexorable,
indifferent, hopeless war
with age, decline, decay.

Was 'if' the product of malign intent
or idle curiosity, to see, while you
relieved the boredom that from
omniscience I assume ensues,
what hope might make us think and do?

It's just not, given what
omnipotence makes possible,
creation of a universe of infinite proportions,
which you with boundless profligacy it seems
left almost empty, worthy of a God.

Nor is it worthy to conceal your purpose
and the meaning of it all
in an elaborate disjunction
at arbitrary intervals delivered randomly
of half sent messages and deeply obscure truths.

Of evil in the world less said the better:
we might accept man's wickedness slipped through
the gate beneath the skirts of choice
but surely you alone must take, for sickness
and all nature's fits of rage, the blame.

Of course there's much that's good –
but not enough. So pick, that we,
deeply unhappy with your management,
may understand, out of the gripes of everyone,
before all turns to dust, the bones.

GOD
"While you fret
don't forget,
I alone
thought to put
mind in matter,
love in life,
flesh on bone.

"I'm the power
and the glory:
that's it,
end of story."

Why

If I was God and I was bored,
I'd make a world much like our own
and people it with folks like us
so I should never feel alone.

I'd give them lives like ours to live
with lots of joy and lots of pain;
through all the ups and downs of life
'twould be their lot to entertain.

I'd watch them every chance I had,
know every character by name
but I would never interfere
for fear that I should spoil the game.

In time I might grow fond of some,
and they in turn might wonder why,
if, through God's love, they'd come to live,
why, through God's will, they had to die:

but die they must, without a doubt,
each of their breath I would deprive
for sadly death is one sure means
to keep a faltering plot alive.

If I was God and I was bored,
I'd make a world much like our own
and people it with folks like us
so I should never feel alone.

Not being God but being me
it seems to me God stands accused
of using me and all of us
simply to keep himself amused.

Surely a shocking thing to do
however lonely He might be,
but worst of all, I'd do it too
if I as lonely felt as He.

Prayer to the Lord

Our Father,
which art in heaven,
what, on earth, was your game?
Why send your son,
your only son? In what way did
his death make us even,
given we put a crown of thorns on his head?
Why did you not simply forgive us our trespasses?
We find it hard to forgive those who trespass against us.
Were you not tempted simply
to deliver us from evil?
After all, thine is the Kingdom
the power and the glory
for ever, whatever.
Amen

Given time

That out of nothing something comes
belies the maths of other sums,
suggesting nought, far less than small,
amounts to something after all.

If we accept what's here is here,
'though what is here remains unclear,
how, out of all this inert splurge,
could what we know as 'life' emerge?

Yet odder still, we have to tell
how from a single living cell
chance – random, purposeless and blind –
knocked out the template of the mind.

A simple message now is taught –
from nought through dust and cell to thought.
From slime to Mozart in his prime
is just what happens, given time.

It's really difficult to see
how all this fits with entropy.
I sometimes feel the need to query
'survival of the fittest' theory.

'O flightless, feathered reptile, strive
for aeons just to stay alive,
not knowing those long finger things
will in the end support your wings.'

OK. No quibbling. Here we find
the stuff of things and life and mind,
unplanned, unwanted, undesigned.

Yet here's a thought on which to muse,
a question reason can't refuse –
how is it more from less ensues?

At least please try to tell me why
life should exist and multiply.
Why should a virus of no use
commit itself to reproduce?

Why should a single cell decide
its role in life was to divide;
and then combine for all its worth
to promulgate all life on earth?

"That's just the way it is, my friend"
is not an answer I'd defend.
Is it not really rather odd
to favour chance instead of God?
You call all God-believers fools
but they at least explain the rules.

"What rules?" you ask in feigned surprise.
The rules that govern seas and skies
and time and space and all we know –
whence came the rules that make it so?

"You really do not understand:
the rules inhere – they are not planned;
much less bestowed by a creator,
a notion that occurred much later.

"It's simple really, evolution
affords a rational solution;
Evolution gives a stir
and makes things better than they were."

That's no more cogent, I'd suggest,
than simply saying 'God knows best'.
Indeed, apart from change of name,
it's saying very much the same.

I'm having trouble I confess
with this idea of more from less.
It will be seen as rather tragic
if science starts to sound like magic.

And when you say the rules "inhere"
I have no doubt you are sincere;
You sound as though you're sure you're sure
but what you mean remains obscure.

Are you suggesting from the start
the rules that govern all formed part
of some primeval churning drum
of hydrogen and helium?
It's not my nature to deride
but where did all the rules reside?

Nor is it I'm so keen on God
(He's often seemed an evil sod)
but if you wish to steal his glory
you need a more compelling story.

The God in whom the faithful trust
turns every devotee to dust;
you need to tell me, if you can,
what magic turned dust into man.

So there you are

So there you are, my god, my god,
as clear as day, as day is fair.
You are not hidden as I thought
but evident in everywhere.

Like water knowing how to lie
yet how to drift up to the sky,
there is nowhere you hide your face.
I see you now in every place.

Like blazing, golden mountain clouds
that glorify the setting sun,
it's very clear to me that you
are not concealed from anyone.

Like gulls that wheel without a care
both slave and master of the air,
they show with secular delight,
your presence in their faultless flight

As trees in serried ranks parade
in perfect order as I pass,
I see you clear in all there is,
no longer darkly through a glass.

Before, dear reader, you conclude
that I'm with godly grace imbued
I think it best I should define
the nature of this god of mine.

I need to make it very clear
this god I see is mine not yours;
he does not ask me to believe
– no sea of faith laps on my shores.

There is no need at all to please
this god with prayer on bended knees.
He does not ask I spend my days
in endless, sycophantic praise.

> "I am the fire that warms and burns,
> and water that slakes thirst or drowns
> I am the breath of life, when roused,
> lays waste whole villages and towns."

Since he accounts for all that is,
the bad as well as good is his;
he occupies no moral state –
his raison d'être to create.

> "I am the rain that quickens seed
> but, when in flood, leaves land defiled;
> I am the sun that fathers life
> but in the end consumes its child.
>
> "I am the god of birth and youth,
> of beauty, clarity and truth
> I am the author of dismay,
> despondency, despair, decay."

There is no way a God of love
would take the trouble to devise
ebola, smallpox, leprosy
and melanoma of the eyes.

No loving God would break earth's crust
to bury legions in the dust,
nor cast a child with damaged mind
into the world, deaf, dumb and blind.

You make excuses for your God:
"Arcane, mysterious but fair."
You're wrong. He's not inscrutable;
it's simply that he doesn't care.

My god at least to me makes sense.
He is a god without pretence;
he is not cruel, is not kind,
– at heart a pure, creative mind.

My god exists in everything,
in every place is always near;
This is the dreadful truth: your God
is hope triumphant over fear.

So if we need a loving God,
we must, and this is surely odd,
create this God as best we can
out of the very best of man.

And if you feel a need to praise
a being resident above,
give thanks this God gave you and me,
despite His faults, the chance to be
a creature capable of love.

This is how God is made

Why should the God who made the world
decide to hide?
What need for secrecy?

Great minds can simple be and that's for sure;
it is our malady.
Great minds entangled in the mesh of time
and disillusioned with the God of old,
confused, have traded God for chance,
upending the old pyramid of thought
to balance it upon its point.

It may be clever but it will not stand.

It's likely true that only a most inefficient God
would take some fifteen thousand million years
to bring us to our present pass.
But it's less plausible by far to any honest mind
that matter undirected
with only random movement as its aid
can substitute for God.

Blind chance is blind, not one to lead the way,
not one to see the way when way there is.

Great minds that cannot see the trees for wood
(or how all evil in the end concedes to good
not vanquished by the armies of the Lord
but trivialised, time after time,
by endless, tedious repetition),
must surely simple be.

What better way to spend the time than making God?
From each of us so little good –
but only good endures;
all that is evil dies as it is born.
This is the verdict men must fear.
The good men do lives after them, all else,
the greed and spite, the lust and the despair,
the little failures and the great betrayals,
all, however noxious, all, all forgiven,
not out of kindness or divine compassion
but because
they are without significance
of no account
dissolved like mist before the rising sun.

This is the judgement all must fear,
the ever-lasting damnation of the lost-for-ever opportunity,
peremptory dismissal
into oblivion
of most of each of us.

This is the meaning of death.
This is how good conquers evil.
This is how love redeems.

This is how God is made.

Rust

Take time with me to ponder this.

A weary wanderer upon an empty shore
braced by the breeze that comes in from the sea
looks down and sees a watch upon the sand.

What does he think?

Perhaps "What luck! I'm having that."

But no. Let us assume
he has a questioning mind.
He studies curiously the watch's face;
It is predictably familiar for it's a face
he's looked at several times a day
for many years.
The hands suggest to him the hand of man.
But more than that, he thinks for sure
that watch was made, as well as worn, by man,
most probably a watch-maker. Oh, yes.

The watch is magic and can speak.
(Just humour me.)
It gives our beach-comber the gift of time.
Now he is blessed with immortality
but, as is common in such tales,
the watch imposes one condition.
If he should ever wish to leave the beach,
he must perform one simple task –
to deconstruct the watch
and put it back together.

He takes the watch apart most carefully,
undoing every tiny screw, releasing every spring,
which he can do
for happily he never wanders on the beach
without his trusty penknife
with its many useful tools,
including a small screwdriver,
much favoured by the army of the Swiss.

He holds a hundred different pieces in his hand.
He's careful not to drop even the smallest part.
He's made a mental note of every step
that he will need to put the watch together
for he is very keen he should not spend
eternity upon this windswept, lonely beach.

"There's one more thing," the watch's voice declares,
(the watch itself no longer being a coherent whole
and capable of speech).
"To make the watch once more a working timepiece,
all you can do is toss the pieces in the air
and hope they come together as before."

"Don't be ridiculous!" declares our friend.
"You know that can't be done."

The watch's voice seems somewhat hurt.
"It's not impossible" the voice insists,
"for that is how I came to be.
Sure, it took time
but, making you immortal,
allows you time enough."

"What makes you think that you were made
by tossing bits and pieces in the air?"
asks our immortal comber of the beach.
"Who made the bits and pieces that were tossed?
Who did the tossing?
And who the hell would want a watch,
except a man who needs to tell the time?

"Look, I don't make the rules," the watch's voice replies.
"You want to master time and live for ever,
take my advice. Start tossing."

The man now shrugs and shakes his head.
"I don't have time for this," he says
and throws the hundred pieces
into the waves that lap the lonely beach.

The waves roll back and forth.
And lo!
the pieces of the watch
rust.

From a Christian to his Islamist brother

Let's agree that,
at the very most,
there is but one God.

But, before you clasp my hand
and greet me as a brother,
I need to make it clear
that my one God
is not the same
as your one God.

My God,
I have to say,
is nothing like your God.

My God is a benign creative power
that nurtures and reciprocates
love,
that's what He does,
gives love for love.

My God reveals to me
that evil thrives on evil
and, hard as it may seem,
the only way to take it down
is to respond with good.

My God requires me to think,
to wrestle with life's mysteries,
to keep an open mind,
to listen, learn and speak the truth;
not to despise or kill
any who disagree.

My God is a forgiving God,
and always merciful.
He extends to me the hand of kindness
of comfort in the times of sadness
and his good fellowship
in all the days of joy.

My God would not condone
the murdering of innocents
in any circumstances;
much less
take the offenders into heaven
and reward them with pleasures of the flesh.
(for sure, more likely
a rather nasty adolescent fantasy
than revelation of the will of God.–
or worse, a cynical device by men
to lure impressionable and naive lads
to sacrifice their lives.)

No God, not mine or any God
deemed worthy of the name,
would take it on Himself to pimp,
oblivious to the wishes of the girls,
some seventy virgins
just to satisfy the lust
of each new murdering martyr.

My God, the creator of both men and women,
would never set the value
of half his greatest work on earth,
full half of humankind,
at half the value of the other half.

And if, from time to time, I lose my faith
He does not panic, much less demand
that I be punished. He's not diminished
by my doubt. My God is perfectly secure,
and not at all offended if,
from time to time,
I find it hard to keep my faith
in truths I cannot always see.

Your God reminds me far too much
of that grotesque god of the Israelites,
vengeful, spiteful and vindictive
a tribal god, not one for all mankind,
quite clearly the creation,
not the creator,
of the human mind,
an attempt, perhaps, to give a modest tribe
a sense of purpose
and superiority.

My God is God of the eternal present;
your God, it seems to me,
is stumbling in the sands of long ago.

My God is so much better than I am.
Your God to me seems worse.

This is a cause for sadness.
Your faith should take its place
as one of the great comforts for humanity
but only when its message
is addressed
not merely to a desert people
locked in the brutish tribal customs
of centuries ago
but to all men and women of goodwill
in every place, at every time.

And given there's one God
and only one,
it's obvious to me
that one of us,
(I try to keep an open mind)
has badly failed to understand,
(for reasons not entirely obscure
given the account above)
what He expects of us.

I would that God

THE CURIOUS UNBELIEVER
    I would that God would stand and spare
    a minute, just to prove He's there.

GOD
    "How can I *stand* and spare a *minute*?
    I'm outside space and time, not in it."
    So even though I deeply care
    I am not part of 'when' and 'where'
    which circumscribe the lives you lead;
    yet give the time and space you need
    to wonder how things came to be
    made by a God you cannot see.
    and of whom most are unaware.

THE CURIOUS UNBELIEVER
    It still seems cruelly unfair
    that we can't know if you are there.

GOD
    What can I say? I fear you must
    take much of what I am on trust.
    But please believe this much is true –
    nothing will shake My faith in you.

Hope

This then I swear

This then I swear.
I will not keep
my dreams for sleep,
for those who do
live in their dreams
and sleep their lives away.
We visit God on mountain tops
not dozing in a valley.

Let not, because of danger, fear and pain,
us drug our souls; nor yet again
because the earth supports
let us not fix our eyes upon
our feet, forgetting that we
stand upon our feet to bring our eyes
a little closer to the skies.

And if there were no sky
we have imagination and a will
which can invent such things
and then insist
till you and I and all the world
know they exist.

Let not, for fear of anarchy or shame,
us grovel for the truth
in little mounds of averages
and piles of notes on what
we at our least can do,
untouched by striving to create and face
something above the common place.

I will not keep
my dreams for sleep,
for those who do
live in their dreams
and sleep their lives away.
We visit God on mountain tops
not dozing in a valley.

This ancient earth of ours is fair

The open road
– silk-smooth and white;
the sun and wind
– saffron delight;
a sky of blue
bright, clear and free;
– as naked swimmers
in the sea

we breathe the gentle April air
and, for a moment, are aware,
this ancient earth of ours is fair.

Cool tables
where companions meet
and laughter sits
by every seat;

then, for a moment,
here and there,
the world exempts
itself of care.

This is offered, this we eat,
drink the wine
blood-warm and sweet,
released, relaxed, renewed, replete.

Young, old, alike, forget the night,
suffused and solaced by the light;
none can take and no one gives;
caught in the instant as it lives.
We breathe the gentle April air
and, for a moment, are aware
this ancient earth of ours is fair.

Voice of life

Anger
kindles,
burns
deep,
flames
leap.

Be tinder
make fire,
but tender;
rage flame
but below
glow
kinder;
in the warm
no harm.

So sad
this is all,
all mad
tears fall;
eyes weep,
let it be
still they see.

Unkind
unfair
worse than these
despair,
one way,
all old,
chill now,
soon cold.

Still small voice
of love
of life
in the fire,
water,
cold,
in and through
and though
still and small
make the choice
now and then
through the years
choose all:
cry above
sounds of strife
use your voice
voice of love
voice of life.

After all

We hear the children laughing
and it seems they have a vision
we have lost;
but is it not the answer
they believe we have
enables them to play?

A young girl's beauty
has such confidence;
is she at peace?
or is her truth
the love her lover,
seeking solace, brings?

An ancient man
his face adorned with lines
of joy and sorrow
sits alone
with dignity.
Yet is his world,
where meaning was
merely a memory
of what he sought,
with that he never found it
all forgotten?

The games must end
and, in the end,
love and memory fail:

the children learn
with age
the ignorance of parents
shall be visited on them;

the young girl and her lover lie
side by side
and think again;

the ancient man
must face about,
set down the comfort of the past
and walk in step with time.

These things are so.
Yet children laugh,
and still the girl is beautiful;
throughout the old man keeps his dignity.

And all this, after all.

Love distilled

Love distilled, refined, immense and vague,
worried and wearied by the wandering of these wasteful ways,
disturbed, distraught, dissatisfied by what before could please,
articulated in the failed image, the exhausted phrase;
give me a god to pray to or take away the need to pray;
stand still, stand firm, stand by me, despite the dwindling of the day;
return and yet retain the strength I give to you to fight,
steady my hand to shape some truth out of the clinging clay.
I work within and through the wakeful silence of the night:
soon shall the god, if god there be in me, in me declare the light.

LIFE

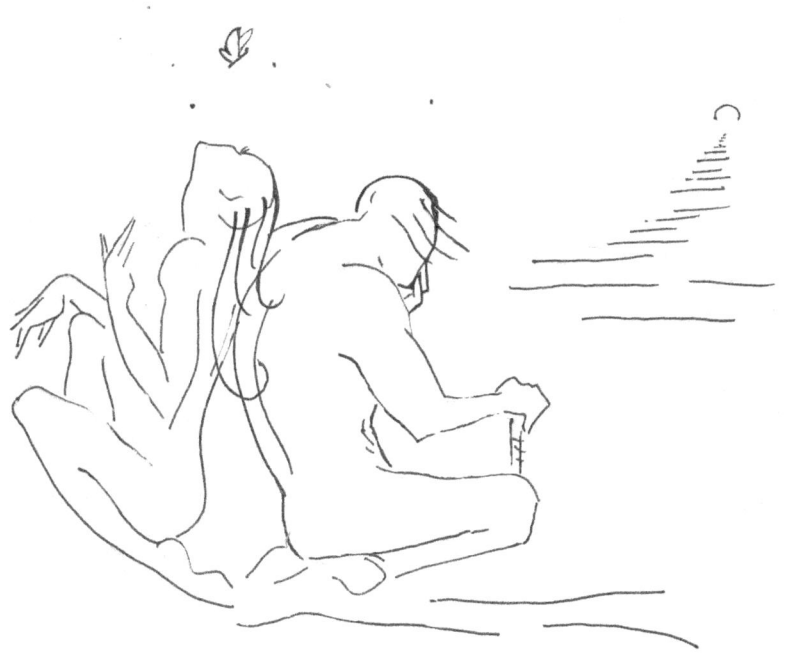

Life's elements

A man, in every circumstance
should learn to take delight
in any thing that can provide
an isolated insight of
the elements of life.

And if, through life's exigencies,
a man should lose his mind,
or give it up to other men
and sadly see his soul decline
in triviality,

then any man who could foresee
his final loss of sight
would probably anticipate
the subtle failing of the light
out of necessity;

and then, in such a circumstance,
he'd surely take offence
at anything that compromised
the undisputed precedence
he should accord without restraint
his isolated insights of
the brightness of life's elements.

One should never leave one's home

One should never leave one's home
on a fine and sunny day:
walks in woods are quite delightful
if you never lose your way.

I went walking one fine morning,
saw a hut with roof of thatch:
three board door and hanging badly
gently, gently, raise the catch.

Enter, blimey! what a hovel,
half the world's unwanted junk:
pots and plaster, wine and crutches
table, broom, a broken bunk:

surprised an urn and contraceptives
never thought such things would mix:
in a chair an aged being
and above a crucifix.

"Tell me, tell me, aged veteran,
you who've been in many wars,
when the sun is shining brightly
why you sit behind closed doors.

"Oh, I'm sure you know the answers
and could tell me many things:
what you've lived for, what you'll die for,
why all beggars are not kings.

"Yes, you're old and wrinkled now
but I'd say you had your day:
took the garter and the stocking
of a virgin in the hay.

"Drained your glass and drained another
women had their fill of you:
here, in darkness, teach the things that
sickness tells old age are true.

"Tell me, tell me, learned master
crowned with thorns about your head.
Tell me, damn you, silent, are you?"
Then he looked and smiled and said:

"One should never leave one's home
on a fine and sunny day;
walks in woods are quite delightful
if you never lose your way."

What might I do!

When people babble through the day
And clocks nag through the night,
when time declares "There's this to pay,"
and you've no coin and cannot say:
"Take what is yours, by you begot,
and then leave me," – (leave you to what?)
"What might I do!" You'd waste the day
by joining those who babble on
until the light of day has gone
and shadows fall before despair.
When sheets drink sweat of love and prayer,
as darkness softly takes all sight,
what urges then this pregnant 'might'?
Listen to clocks nag through the night?

Venus arose

Venus arose, while Mars was yet abed.
Nimbly she slipped from sheets with leap ethereal,
Carelessly combed the locks upon her head,
Swiftly prepared the tea, the toast and cereal,
Dressing she thought how she would spend each hour
Laundry and shopping, all delights venereal:
Mars then emerged to plan beneath a shower
Deeds that promote a hero managerial.

Such are the days in which the gods abound –
She keeping clean the halls of heaven;
He fighting monsters in the underground,
Returning weary but victorious, at seven:
    If these be not the myths in which we hide,
    I never writ nor no man ever lied.

Even a busy urban man

Even a busy urban man may find
the number of his years begins to weigh
upon the concrete structures of his mind,
his balance sheet not red, nor black, but grey:
the coming day will bring him no relief,
provide for him no colourful event
of joy to break the monotone of grief
for assets he has neither saved nor spent.

And yet he laughs and rises from his bed,
girds up his loins to face the routine strife,
places his bowler helmet on his head,
grips firm his brolly, like a Spartan knife,
and, with the bravery of heroes dead,
plucks for his buttonhole the flower of life.

The measurements of man

They lied beyond all limit when
they took the measurements of man
and noted only length and breadth
to fit their plain descriptive plan.

But what I cannot understand
is why we listened to their lies;
would we entrust a building to
an architect with glass for eyes?

With measurements they circumscribed
the object of their scrutiny
and built a coffin strong enough
to quell a doubtful mutiny.

We shall rebel without revenge,
and take no pleasure in their cries;
it is enough that they should know
the thing they buried shall arise.

This and that

That man who limps
looks in a glass
and postures gracefully;
catching at straws for gold.

This woman, having been beautiful,
longs for the time when
no man can look at her
and think, in his own way,
of then and now;
catching at straws for gold.

That girl – this her first time –
thinks of nothing
for the last time, having learned
nothing so well this night;
catching at straws for gold.

And the old man on that bench
leaning forward, watches passers by
and fondly dreams of
the youth and health that
drained him to an old skin;
catching at straws for gold.

Somewhere young or old
a shattered body or exhausted mind
acts out the 'last denial' –
this too
catching at straws for gold.

Of course many another lives
having learned
gold is not for men
only tinsel
on the cloaks of gods;
and that
all may look on the sun setting
paint the sea, or the burnished field of
daffodils – then catch no more,
– and this the last straw.

Uncertainty

If I had been
before I was,
before my birth,
and you had said,
before I was,
that I would be
upon this earth,,
I would have said,
had I a tongue,
it cannot be.

If you were now
to say to me,
now I am here
and fit and young
that I will be
when I'm no more,
I'd tend to say
it cannot be –
but now perhaps
I'm not so sure.

And if it is
that I persist
when others think
I am no more,
then I surmise
that future life
will likely be
as great a leap
as great surprise
as this, my life,
has proved to be
from anything
that went before.

The twig

The twig that falls
throughout its fall
precisely fits
the space it occupies.

Of all the worlds
I can create
within the virtual orb
of my mind's eye
there's none
as tight and closed
and quite precise
as this arrangement
of the falling twig
and the commensurate space
it occupies
at every instant
as it descends to earth.

Sleep

I sleep, I cease to be:
without a thought
I take the chance
of losing me.

Unless I dream.

Within my dreams
an 'I' not me
inhabits a reality
that lives a thousand
different lives:
it has no substance
yet is all
that in my sleep
keeps hope alive
that 'me' survives.

That 'me' that when
the morning breaks
awakes and takes
the past and makes
out of my wakeful memory
the thing I like to think is me.

Unless I dream.

A kind deceit

Who told the child that cried
all would be well?

There is a kind deceit
played by a parent on a child
that opens up a gap as wide
as the divide
that separates hope from despair
and truth from lies.

Who said that being older
makes you wise?
Who told the child that cried
all would be well,
when he or she who spoke
knew well enough they lied?

Tears dried, the child then smiled,
not knowing, when full grown
and parent to its own,
it would seem better far to lie
or not to tell the truth
than let the truth be known.

These hollow gods who strut
on childhood's stage
cannot assuage
the fears that make mere mortals weep.
Yet still they give wild promises
they know they cannot keep.

Dry leaves, wizened, lifeless

Dry leaves, wizened, lifeless,
scurry on the vast and
oceanic blasts of air.
    Why cling to a tree?
Let the forked branches stretch
naked,
in their agony resist
the forced-satanic heaving wreck.

Drying boughs, branches, twigs,
taut, aching in the wind.
    Trees can't turn their back.
Leaves escape
the sharp cry
of the sudden sky-rape.

Wind-cracked,
Wind-cracked,
The sound drowns,
in titanic gales.

Dry leaves, wizened, lifeless
glory in your freedom,
in the splendid howling pomp;
she who bound you
bore you, and fed you
for the 'greater glory' is humbled.

Others may face firm this storm
and in the Spring burst into
laughter, but not she.
She will dry out like you
only more slowly
and die.
But the wind that tore
and the leaves that fled, dancing
gladly before their new master
have whirled far away
and now bear no glory or gladness.

And the tree has lost its agony, as a man loses interest.

Walls

A man within four walls confined
in comfort will know peace of mind
until his intellect confides
that every wall must have two sides.

The outside soon to him is known;
his second habitat outgrown.

Now is no limit to his pride –
he will not, cannot be denied;
these are the truly golden years
when thoughts of walls are faded fears.

He struts his stuff without a care
until his heart informs his head,
when all is done and all is said,
the other side of hope's despair.

Now wisdom, bulging like a sack,
lies heavy on his aching back;
advice he offers, no-one takes,
for each prefers his own mistakes;
the tales he tells of days of yore,
too often told, become a bore;
adventure and the call to roam
seem less attractive than his home.

Once more within four walls confined,
he finds a kind of peace of mind.
He sits beside a homely fire
warmed by the embers of desire,
knowing those walls that used to chafe
are only there to keep him safe.

Rambling

When I was young
or, rather, had less years than now
for I am still not old,
(let's settle for less time to extricate the way of things),
I thought,
(though "I" is problematical
since I remember thinking
but the "I" of now is rather different from the "I" of then)
could it be possible
that anyone could spend a life
in seeking to acquire?
Where was the point, what satisfaction
could there be in gathering
the artefacts of life?
A futile exercise, it seemed to me,
an endless quest,
a task without a goal.

I also saw injustice in the way the world was run.
Why was it that, with equal effort,
unequal shares ensued?
A chance of birth made one man rich for life
another poor however hard he worked.
An accident of birth could give a surfeit
of life's blessings
or such insufficiency that, in some far off land,
a mother must decide which child should die
that others of her brood might live.

Please don't misunderstand. Such thoughts
still resonate with me. I still believe,
amidst the clutter of my life,
(acquired, at least in part, to fit
the pattern of the present times)
that wealth should be the natural consequence
of merit. (Before you interrupt, of course I see
a modest shift in emphasis from effort
to the concept of desert
but, after all, effort misplaced is unproductive,
scarcely conducive to the common good,
and therefore undeserving.)

I still believe that any life
devoted to the acquisition
of what the world deems valuable
is insufficient, of itself, to justify
the living of a life.

But now, being older and, I hope,
much wiser than the callow youth
who troubles me with fading recollections of
a distant, disconnected past,
the logic of the way we live
seems strong enough to me,
as I now am,
to keep the world in place.

It's easy when you have no wealth
to hold it in contempt,
or argue vehemently
for equal shares.
Strangely, when wealth is redistributed,
it simply tends to alienate the rich
and inculcate in those who benefit
still greater discontent.

You quibble with this view
and pick me up, quite rightly,
on "simply tends."
"Simple," you say, it surely isn't
and I'll concede. I used it merely
as a rhetorical device,
(just as I just used "merely".)
As for "tends," I slipped it in
for fear that you might cite
some poor deserving case where
better diet or a place to live
engendered gratitude.

Your smile suggests you think that I am rambling,
to which I must reply
I should make faster progress
with fewer interruptions on the way.

The essence of my argument is this:
if I now met that strangely alien youth
that I once was,
I'd say to him the very things
that I, when I was him, held in contempt.

And I am left to ponder whether
in the intervening years
I have grown wiser
(which, on mature reflection, seems
the only rational view)
or whether, in the passing of my life,
I have grown deaf to arguments
that once were sound –
and blind to what was then,
or so I thought some thirty years ago,
the truth.

A father's song

I am the creator
omnium pater.
For my delight
into being I brought you,
    male and female.

While you two were still young,
I sang my strong song,
both day and night;
with true tones I taught you,
    male and female?

When it came to the day
of your turning away
as was your right,
still fearsome I fought for you,
    male and female.

Unfettered, free to go,
yes, you I saw grow,
stunned by the sight
of your grafting and giving,
    male and female.

You are not mine, for sure.
but know I am yours,
trapped, shackled tight
in the net of your living,
    male and female,

I am the creator,
omnium pater.
I am the long light,
loving, lauding, forgiving,
omnium pater,
created creator,
first son, then father
for now and forever,
    my son and my daughter.

Sum ergo sum

I am, therefore I am.

There is no need for thinking.
Before the thought, do you not see
there is an *I* to think?

Nor is there any need for therefore,
pace Descartes
I am, I am, I am.

What is this *I*
precursor of all thought
precursor of the things I think upon,
servant and master of the senses that I use,
informant and informer of the other,
the other being all that is not *I*?

Some say it is the sum
of what my senses tell me,
of all that I experience and all that I recall
But that's not it or, at the least, not all of it.
On top of that there is the *I*
that knows that I am me;
the watcher, witness, critic
of all that I experience,
the ponderer of life,
the poet, painter,
composer, creator,
the maker of more from less;
the very *I* of knowing I am me.

Of course this *I* is both a gift and curse,
an immaterial entity
ensnared within a plethora of things:
I am the god who urinates;
the angel who excretes;
And I am also
the primate who abandons
the branches of a tree
to feel the ecstasy
of Handel's Alleluia chorus;
the dust born of, and reacher for, the stars

I am is indisputable.
And curled up in *I am*
is everything that I have been,
and seen and done –
my memories;
but, more than that,
(and this requires thought so deep it hurts)
I am is everything that I have made
of all my memories,
and what those memories have made of me
and what I have forgotten,
and what, if anything, I brought with me
before there was *I am*.

What is the meaning of *I am*?
That is the question *I am* poses
to every *I* who is.
What is my purpose,
what is the purpose of *I am*?
Why am I *I am*?
What is the truth?

Nothing is certain except this.
Truth, if it exists, is over-rated.
I am does not need truth;
I am must search for meaning
but meaning is not something to be found.
Meaning is made,
as *I am* made.
As I am made
I am.

The sentence of life

It starts, a cold, blank, empty stare;
no marker yet shows anywhere.
We search for characters in vain
across the endless alban plain.

The journeyman looks to the east,
fear diminished, hope increased.
Dawn lights the land. Now all he sees
are endless possibilities.

Through instinct, he will understand
that every venture must be planned
for where he puts his foot will tend
to point towards the journey's end.

He steps on to the bright, white snow,
his heart now set on where to go.
Let him take care or he may find
the light or cold distracts his mind.

He may not know but at his back
the prints he makes define his track.
His options dwindle, day by day,
as he pursues his chosen way.

He cannot pause, he must move on,
even should all hope be gone,
for once the journey is begun
time sets the pace for everyone.

Each further stride commits his soul
to head towards his chosen goal.
Each choice eliminates *per force*
the chance to take a different course.

His destination, now so near,
remaining choices disappear.
Now all can see that he at last
can add no future to the past

It's only when his race is run
when all that he can do is done,
when all his past is firmly sealed,
that the whole picture is revealed

Then we can judge without dissent
the essence of each incident,
what was the drive, the true intent,
and what, if anything, it meant.

Cause, effect, time and broken rhymes

We see effects and think we know,
for each, some cause has made it so.
But here's a thought to give us pause –
the effect is curled up in the cause.
We think: "First, cause; and then effect,"
but if you look you will detect,
cause and effect are one at heart.
It's only time keeps them apart.

So when we aim and throw the dart
where it will journey from the start,
its entire flight, where it will land,
is present in the throwing hand.
It's time alone that intervenes
to fabricate sequential scenes;
it makes a break where there is none;
the cause and caused are clearly one.

Which leads me on to ponder time,
a concept surely past its prime!
If time is real, how can it be
that 'now' and 'then' fit perfectly?
What guarantees that 'this' today
will link with 'that' of yesterday?
If time can be both slow and fast,
what holds the future to the past?

And if time's arrow took a turn
and backwards ran, we'd have to learn,
when making plans and setting goals,
cause and effect had swapped their roles.
We'd look at an effect and see
that it had caused the cause to be,
which means, when all is said and done,
cause and effect are really one.

Time is at root a deep enig-
ma, but most probably a fig-
ment of a greatly troubled ment-
al state of endless discontent-
edness. Thus time takes life and cru-
dely cuts what we should see is tru-
ly one more than a thousand times,
leaving a trash of paradigms,
much like this verse of broken rhymes,
of rhythm casually ignored
of ideas only half-explored,
and now, the puzzled reader whines,
a stanza with too many lines.

The unexamined life

It's obvious to anyone who thinks.
We wander in the no-man's-land between
the body and the mind, bonded by links
which clearly force the sacred and obscene
to jostle, side by side, along life's tracks.
While worlds of thought slip past behind our backs,
we sate our hunger, avarice and lust,
and pass from birth, mostly bemused, to dust.

Of course it's not impossible to spend
a lifetime at the body's beck and call.
But what a waste! There really is no end
to what the body wants. It wants it all.
    So Socrates, he of the nagging wife,
    wisely condemned an unexamined life.

We smuggled love into the world

Today I'm going to share with you
a secret that will break your heart.
I'll prove there's nothing you can trust;
the things that you believe are true
are now about to fall apart.
Each dream you have will turn to dust

Entrapped within a self, alone,
thinking the world we know is real,
most voyage on a ship of fools.
The sails flap, the timbers groan;
there is no captain at the wheel.
The sea and wind impose the rules.

I'm not a mean, vindictive man,
'though some might choose to disagree.
I have a truly noble goal
a clearly well-intentioned plan
wholly benign as you will see
to make what's broken once more whole.

But first I need to make it plain;
all things you touch and think are real
are far less solid than they seem.
You look surprised. Let me explain
the wood and stone you think you feel
are less substantial than a dream.

And you yourself, I'm sad to tell,
are far from what you think you are.
Prepare yourself for a surprise.
For every single human cell
there's ten times more bacteria
within the body you comprise.

But there's no need to be depressed.
The universe, famed for its size,
of which you think you are aware
was once, they tell me, so compressed
that, microscoping with your eyes,
you would have sworn it wasn't there.

So here we are, in fear and doubt,
misled in almost every way
by what our puny senses glean.
Appalled we see there's no way out;
we ask but not a soul can say
what all this mystery might mean.

Do not lose heart. There is good news.
Your brain which weighs a mere three pounds
and is, no doubt, both boon and curse,
can find a way, should you so choose,
to burst beyond diurnal bounds
and comprehend the universe.

O what a piece of work is man
whose thoughts can ride upon the wind,
can scud across the widest sea;
can chart a course, concoct a plan.
There is no ban he can't rescind
if he's a mind to set us free.

We have the power, if we dare,
to fly the ship across the sky
to unknown lands, mainsail unfurled.
And should we meet with cold despair,
face mockery and insults hurled,
we've one success none can deny,
'though those with blinkered minds may try,
an answer to the question why,
we smuggled love into the world.

The first mistake

The game is done, the die is cast;
the chains, corroded, break at last.
With open mind, I clearly see
how blind they are who are not free.

Of course when trapped in daily dross,
we pay our dues to wear and tear.
We face the pain of age and loss
and whine that life is most unfair.

For sure, it cannot be denied
by anyone at journey's end –
the body, never satisfied,
is more a tyrant than a friend.

* * *

Now lazing on a fresh cut lawn
untrammelled by a core of care,
I am, to my surprise, reborn
although I am, and am not, there.

I visit places I have known;
each one now vividly defined.
I somehow make them more my own
than when they were in time confined.

I leave the land at break of day
to scud across the ocean spray;
the salty droplets splash a place
which is, and yet is not, my face.

How can I see the land and skies
without the benefit of eyes?
I find it hard to understand
how I can touch without a hand.

The senses I relied upon
which told me everything I knew,
I now can see, now they are gone,
distorted and obscured my view.

At last an end to guilt and fear;
there is no sentence to rescind.
Towards the mountains now I steer
and ride upon the midnight wind.

How is it out of less comes more?
The world I thought to leave behind
is so much closer than before.
Now it and I are of one mind.

And, courtesy of human wit,
a thought can easily survive
the body that engendered it
when foresaid body was alive.

All things that make a life worthwhile,
love, friendship, laughter and a smile,
the things that nothing can replace,
were never ruled by time and space.

And as for love, my love for you
was, is and always will be prime
and certainly not subject to
the mindless, wheedling tick of time.

The good we do throughout our lives
the best of us, is what survives.
What I now am abjures the night,
and soars with ease into the light.

The sleep is past; at last awake
the mind, embracing all, is free.
I realise my first mistake
was thinking that the I was me.

Occasional Poems

Essay on man and woman
To mark the wedding of my son Josh to Jessica

The bride requested I take time
to decorate my thoughts with rhyme,
to share the wisdom of my life
with those now joined as man and wife.

Each day for years in lengthy sessions,
I've wrestled with life's toughest questions.
Aware, aghast, often alone,
I've chewed life's existential bone.

So it should come as no surprise
to learn that I'm exceeding wise;
and in these lines I hope to show
there's very little I don't know.

While Socrates had to confess
as he grew older, he knew less;
I'm proud to say that, on that score,
as I've grown older I know more.

'Tis said, pride comes before a fall
but, truth to tell, I know it all.
What's more I'm now prepared to share
my wisdom with this happy pair

So here's a start, which Josh derides,
know every sausage has four sides;
This is a culinary law
for all who don't like sausage raw;
a rule, when sadly overlooked
means sausages served undercooked,
or worse, unless this lesson's learnt,
both undercooked and badly burnt.

Accept things change throughout your lives.
Enjoy what is, while it survives.
Delight in life at every stage
but never fear to turn the page.
As Heraclitus used to say
"All is in flux" or πάντα ρει
    So carpe diem (seize the day);
    then let what's dwindling fade away.

Be optimistic Those are cursed
who always choose to think the worst.
What others as a setback see
can be an opportunity.
    Be bold, be confident and strong –
    but have plan B in case you're wrong.
If troubles come, devise a plan
to fix the problems that you can;
    Those you can't fix, simply eschew.
    Don't try. Find better things to do.

And if, in business you must choose
a course of action and you lose,
be not dismayed. If you are right
just half the time, you're pretty bright.
And anyone whose score is higher
is bloody lucky or a liar.
     Life is not chess. Make no mistake,
     there's risk in every choice you make.

Know this. No one always succeeds.
To fail is the spur one needs
to learn. Take hard knocks on the chin
and keep on trying till you win.
     It's often true – no one knows why –
     success rewards the final try.

When others envy your success
and see themselves as so much less,
it's not, as humans, out of order
to quaff a tot of schadenfreude.
It's not enough to win; we need
to see our closest rivals bleed.
     But have a care – this could be true –
     one day they'll schadenfreude you.

There's many things you'll want to buy,
hard to resist, I can't deny,
But, pray, beware, for in my view,
possessions end up owning you.
     To break the grip of wanting stuff,
     simply decide you have enough.

Now Josh, if arguing with Jess,
remember this, that more is less;
the more you say, the less success
you'll have in finding happiness.
    The ladies have known all along
    that they are right and we are wrong.

And Jess, if Josh seems not to hear
a clear instruction, do not fear
that he intends to disobey.
It's just his mind is far away,
embroiled in structures so refined
they fully occupy his mind.

And never ever go to bed
with grumpy feelings in your head
Resolve disputes with love and wit
always before you hit the pit.
However busy you may be,
make time to talk. It is the key
to growing closer through the years
of all that living, joy and tears.
In victory or in defeat,
support each other, don't compete.
    Remember, to fulfil each dream
    that, first and foremost, you're a team

And if in time you should be blest
with kids, then know *that is* the best.
    The best thing I have ever done
    was have a daughter and a son.

Know this, true happiness you'll find
in a companion of the mind;
someone who when the harsh winds blow,
or when you freeze in ice and snow,
or when you fight against the tide,
will always be there at your side.
When troubles threaten all you've planned,
they will be there to take your hand.
    There is no force that stands above
    the power of committed love.

That's what we celebrate today.
We wish God speed you on your way
    I speak for all within this room
    Have happy lives …
        the bride and groom.

A father's thoughts
To mark the wedding of my daughter Stephanie to Natalia

I saw you born. You came into this world
with volleys of applause from everyone.
who crowded the theatre of your birth.
to see a brand new life so well begun.

You grew into a child and it was clear
you watched the world with sharpness of intent.
You pieced together all you saw and heard
and, smiling, slyly worked out what it meant.

You took the measure of each task you faced,
determined how much effort you would need,
no more, no less than what you thought required
to quietly, unobtrusively succeed.

And when the girl approached the brave new world
of womanhood, you boldly took the view,
despite residual cant and prejudice
you must and would, to your own self, be true.

Life is a fearsome journey for us all
with challenges and dangers all around,
but you have wit and honesty and will
to face and fight them on your chosen ground.

You showed your mettle in the jobs you took
and did much more than you were paid to do.
Some even tried to break you but they found
they'd bitten off much more than they could chew.

Today starts a new chapter in your life
with someone whom you love and whom you trust.
I tell you, daughter, true love will endure
'though pyramids and castles turn to dust.

What is a father's role in all of this,
with wife and daughter sitting at my side?
I thank my wife for such a wondrous gift
and then look on with pleasure and with pride

The greatest joy in life is to be loved;
it is the light that gifts the heart to see.
Know this, my girl, whatever fate may bring,
you have a father's deepest love from me.

Stories

Ibn Saud

Banished was I from the heart of Arabia,
Riyadh, my home, had been stolen by others;
banished was I, and my father and mother,
brothers and sisters, deprived of our birthright.
Sadness we felt for the years that denied us
the feel of the sand of the Nejd in our hands.

Kindness we found in Kuwait beyond measure
but kindness alone could not cure the pain
of living in exile, a life without pleasure,
for pleasure, not nurtured in honour, will wither.
I knew from the earliest years of my living
that I must return to the place of my birth.

They told me that only my death would await me,
(but fear is a far harsher master than death);
they warned of the dangers of crossing the desert
but it was the desert had given me breath.
They asked how a lad could recapture a city,
when put to the sword what my pride would be worth;
I asked how the seed, lying dry in the sand, at
the first taste of rain can emerge from the earth.

"Who will ride at my side on this perilous venture?
Who will risk life and limb to expel Al Rashid?"
Sixty answered my call, young and brave, one and all.
"With all of our strength, we will give what you need;
we will stand by your side when the battle is joined
until each of us falls – or Riyadh is freed."

It was not for the glory we rode from Kuwait;
we held faith as our shield and justice our sword.
I sought to regain the land of my fathers
but in all I deferred to the will of the Lord.
We rode towards Riyadh with banners unfurled,
putting trust in the God who created the world.

Through a cold Ramadan we encamped in the desert;
we fasted one month in the village of Haradh,
far away from the eyes of those who might think
that folly could lead us to try to take Riyadh.
When the fasting was over, I summoned my kinsmen;
without hesitation they answered my call.
Like shadows that slip over sand dunes at sunset
we gathered in silence beneath Riyadh's wall.

On that night long ago, when the time came to act,
I knew in my heart what it was to be free;
the greatest good fortune in life for a man
is to know he has reached for the best he can be.
Whatever might follow that cold, moonless night
we would know we had fought for a cause that was right.

I chose from my band a mere handful of men;
each one read the risks from the look in my eyes.
We scaled the walls under cover of darkness;
we watched for the sun to put light in the skies.
Outnumbered, we knew that our hope of success
must depend in the end on our use of surprise.

In a fight it is true if you strike off the head
of a man or an army, the battle is won.
We few faced a garrison ready to crush us;
such odds left no question what had to be done.
The fate of the Amir of Riyadh was sealed.
He must die for the wounds of Al Saud to be healed.
When Ajlan, the Amir, appeared in the open,
we struck as the lion descends on its prey.
Bin Jelawi forced open the gate of the fortress;
the rest of our brothers then joined in the fray.
The garrison knew that resistance was futile;
Al Saud had returned to its home on that day.

Looking back through the decades, the taking of Riyadh
was merely one step on a path, hard and long.
After many a battle, I put all my heart into
building a nation, devout, proud and strong,
with justice its sword and faith as its shield,
in the land where the message of God was revealed.

The tortoise and the hare

On a bright summer's day, when the sun was a-roastin',
the animals gathered 'neath the shade of a tree;
and talked of the things they like to do most in
the hours of leisure 'twixt midday and three;
when Harold the Hare, who was given to boastin',
leaped up and declared: "no-one's faster than me."

"So what!" said the Badger: "Who cares if your faster?
"no-one but a madman would run in this heat:
a sprint in this weather would lead to disaster,
in death, or at least in athlete's feet."
"I see" quoth glib Harold, "that I am the master
in matters of running," and returned to his seat.

"I'll be jiggered and joggered," said Stanley Stoat quickly
"if we cannot find someone faster than you."
"I could try," offered Albert. "No, no, you are sickly";
the badger discouraged the brave kangaroo.
"It's true I'm not well," pallid Al replied thickly,
"'Twas the beans I'm convinced in last night's bowl of stew."

"Enough!" cried vain Harold. "Admit you're defeated.
There's no-one can match my extraordinary pace."
"Be quiet," said a voice, "and please remain seated.
Your arrogance really is quite out of place.
I am forced to conclude you're extremely conceited
and suggest that we test your resolve in a race."

The challenge had come from an unlikely quarter,
from a creature not noted for moving at speed.
'Twas Teresa the Tortoise, old Plovis's daughter,
old Plovis, who once in his youth had decreed
that running was something that nobody oughta
engage in unless there was desperate need.

"My word!" sniggered Harold, "unless I'm mistaken
Teresa the Tortoise has gone off her head;
the heat of the sun on her shell must be baking
her brains till they take on the texture of bread;
I hate to see anyone's confidence shaken
but challenging me is simply incred …"

"Desist!" snapped the Badger, "if words could win races,
it's clear you would lead by at least half a mile."
Then he turned to Teresa; "How on earth can you face his
unrivalled speed in so desperate a trial?"
"To see that this rabbit is put in his place is
a dream I hold dear," she replied with a smile.

"A rabbit, a rabbit!" bold Harold exploded:
"how dare you, you ignorant, dull herbivore!
Your reptilian brain has become overloaded;
I'm a hare, not a rabbit. Dammit! never before
have I ever been so unforgivably goaded;
the race is the place where I'll settle this score."

The animals gathered in ones, twos and threes,
(though how you can gather in ones is unclear)
"I'd suggest" quipped the hare, "you all fall on your knees
and pray to Old Plovis (whose name you revere)
that a way may be found to save poor Terese
from the drubbing that everyone knows she must fear."

153

Teresa decided that further debating
was not the most useful employment of time.
"Let the contest begin – no more hesitating.
If you are so sure of your ground speed then I'm
sorely prompted to ask why on earth are we waiting?
This profligate squand'ring of words is a crime."

It is gen'rally known that the practice of betting
is rife amongst badgers and stoats everywhere.
Stanley crunched up some numbers, and after much fretting
declared "10 to 1" was exceedingly fair.
Despite the poor odds which the creatures were getting,
it's not p'raps surprising that most backed the hare.

As challenger, choosing the course they must follow
was a task that Teresa accepted with grace.
"The length of this cornfield to Holly Bush Hollow,
through Cherry Tree Wood, past Farmer Giles' place,
to the edge of the stream, round the old weeping willow,
then back to this tree for the end of the race."

The length of the course seemed to many surprising
in view of the Tortoise's shortness of shin;
but Oswald the Owl, alone realising
the challenger's face bore the trace of a grin,
checked the odds, which young Stanley was just finalising,
and then placed a bet on Teresa to win.

The race had a fairly explosive beginning
for the badger clapped paws in a manner designed
to produce a loud bang; Harold, openly grinning,
set off like a bullet. Teresa, resigned
to a rather less obvious method of winning,
fell further and further and further behind.

So fast ran young Harold, he soon was exceeding
a speed which permitted the ground and his feet
to meet, except briefly, and then only needing
the lightest of touches, a featherlight beat
of his pads, to maintain his phenomenal speeding.
Teresa meanwhile plodded on through the heat.

Now I should p'raps explain that Harold was fonder
of carrots than anyone ever should be;
so it's scarcely surprising he started to ponder
the thought that he might just have time to take tea.
At Farmer Giles' place he declared: "I see yonder
a challenge at last that is worthy of me."

The challenge consisted of quickly consumin'
some freshly dug carrots which lay in a pile
at the side of the farmhouse. "There is no more room in
my tummy," sighed Harold on finishing. "I'll
be blowed if I see any point in resumin'
my place in the race till I've rested a while."

O so slowly and surely Teresa was keeping
her mind firmly fixed on her purpose, invok-
ing the spirit of Plovis, an adept at heaping
misfortune on those who dare foolishly joke
at another's expense. Not for her any sleeping.
She was long past the willow e'er Harold awoke.

"Oh my goodness!" cried Harold, at once realising
he might very soon have to swallow his boast;
"How could I nod off? I'm a fool for despising
a creature inspired by Plovis's ghost."
Harold ran like the wind with a hurricane rising
but the Tortoise, 'though tiring, was first past the post.

"I believe," hooted Oswald with evident pleasure,
"my wager will win me a fiver or more;
it was clear that Teresa had Harold Hare's measure.
Have we not seen him gorging on carrots before?
Poor Harold may now ruminate at his leisure
that faster in short bursts is slower than sure."

"But how could you know," queried Stanley dejected,
"that Harold would stop at Farmer Giles' place?"
"'Twas the course that Teresa so shrewdly selected
that led straight from here to the hare's loss of face.
Last night on a flight I clearly detected
the carrots that hobbled the hare's faster pace."

Now there's always a moral in every good tale
and here we have many which none can gainsay.
Over-eating of carrots can lead you to fail;
take care you can win any bet that you lay;
even when you believe you are sure to prevail
remember that pride is a debt you must pay;
but this most of all, come rain, shine or hail,
as you run life's good race over meadow and dale,
in the hot blood of youth, or when thin blood runs pale,
it is those who try hardest and follow the way
who will surely succeed at the end of the day.

Lyrics

There's a way

There's a way you can pray
at the crack of dawn.
Praise the Lord
that you were ever born,
smile, sing,
let the laughter ring,
see the wonder in everything.

When you stand as you planned
on your plot in the sun,
see the light
shines on everyone.
Look, see,
how the world would be
if we set all the people free.

Raise your eyes to the skies
when the sun sinks low.
See the stars above from
far below,
love, give,
every day you live,
that's the only thing you need to know.

Square One – theme song

The wind wanders by, through the streets of the town,
dark as the night or a tired lover's frown.
Softly it moves over tree tops and roofs,
feeling its way like a lover at play;
and it climbs through the sky, while a lone passer-by,
makes his way, makes his way through the streets of the town.
And his soul is as dark as the frown of the night,
and as blind as the mind of the wind.

I need you to love me,
I need you to love me,
I need as the sun needs the day.
My life is devoured,
By knave, fool and coward,
these shadows with nothing to say.

The wind takes the leaves in the palm of its hand,
murmuring hope of an old promised land.
Gently they fall in the night at its call,
whispering low of the love that they know
they will find, as they fly, with the wind through the sky.
as they dance through the town so in love with the night.
But the wind, it is blind and the dance is misled,
for the leaves that can fly must be dead.

Day of days

In a land long ago
in the deepening winter snow
a young woman and her husband came to crowded Bethlehem.
But no room at the inn
for the woman or her kin;
they must sleep with only animals to warm and comfort them.

In the still of the night
Mary saw a brilliant light
from a star that lit the manger from a winter sky so cold.
Now the hour, now the birth
that forever changed the earth;
Mary knew the time had come that had for so long been foretold.

In the fields near the town
a lone shepherd heard a sound
and a voice not his but near him formed these words upon his breath
"For the child born this day
will drive all your fears away
and the king of life will overcome the very fear of death."

Mighty kings make their way
to the manger where they pray
to this son of God, this son of man, whom no-one can gainsay:
these the gifts they confer
frankincense and gold and myrrh
on this child who, it is certain, shall be greater far than they.

So rejoice one and all
when you hear our Saviour's call;
Christmas brings to each of us a gift that will forever last.
Time to give and forgive.
to enrich the life we live,
For this day is still the day of days, though centuries have passed.

Stuff & Nonsense

Song of the Pongid

I'm a pongpoidal person
and I will not settle for less.
I have hairs upon my buttocks,
I have hairs on my chest.
    And the length of arm
    has a certain charm
as I brachiate about.
I'm a pongpoidal person,
as you'll often hear me shout.

I'm a pongpoidal person
and my name is Mr P.
I'm a hominid who's hirsute,
as hirsute as can be.
    And you'll detect
    the great respect
the world accords to me,
as I ripple through the branches of
a giant jungle tree.

The Pongid lament

Oh! pongipoid!
don't be annoyed.
The world we love has been destroyed.

The sky is grey, the leaves turn brown
and heavy rains are falling down.
Oh! pongipoid
don't be annoyed,
the world we love has been destroyed

Thus winters come and bring the snow.
Yet it must be that winters go.
So, pongipoid,
despite the pain,
the world we lost we'll build again.

And, in the Spring, we both shall sing
how pongids conquer everything.
So, pongipoid,
despite the pain
the world we lost we'll build again.

Paean to Pong

The elephant's skin
is thicker than thin
and his trunk is incredibly long.
But none is so fair
it can bear to compare
with the subtly ineffable Pong.

The gorilla is wise,
of a sensible size
and his arms are surprisingly strong.
But none is so fair
it can bear to compare
with the lithely lubricious Pong.

The arrogant stoat
has a smooth silken coat
that is finer than any sarong.
But none is so fair
it can bear to compare
with the nobly munificent Pong.

O the Pongid has eyes
that are bright as the skies
and she sings such an elegant song.
With her red bushy tail
all comers must fail
to compare with the Pedigree Pong.

In the forests so deep
when men are asleep,
she basks in the lunar reflection,
Then she swings through the trees
with such rubicund ease
– a paean to natural selection.

On the discovery of the Hog's Bison

A physicist pig
took to wife a young cow.
His father said: "Now,
tell me why, son,
when all's said and done,
why go for a cow,
when there's many a sow
you could try, son?"

The young pig replied;
"I thank you, indeed,
for your years of advice
on how best to succeed.
but it's time to confide,
pig to pig, man to man,
I'm consumed by the need
to breed if I can
the thing that no creature has ever laid eyes on,
the thing that all physics has put a high price on,
the essential, but strangely elusive, hog's bison."

Normandy

Faim for le fromage
fancy a peck
Emmental, Beaufort
et Pont l'Evêque.

Appetite jaded
visions in grey
Gaperon, Cantal
ou Fromage Frais.

Walking on plages
cheeks all aglow
Munster, Saingorlon
Chaource, Livarot.

At the end of the journey
at the edge of the sea
the best things in life
are undoubtedly Brie.

Let's pretend

Let's pretend
that the world
is a ball of green,
lost
in the valley of the shadow of death:
and if I
should stand
with legs apart
and scream for the world
like a child from the heart,
then some old fool
deaf, dumb, blind and lame
would give me the ball
for the sake of the game.
But the trouble is
that the world I've seen
is not a ball
though it is partially green,
and it's me and the old fool, both short of breath,
who are lost in the valley of the shadow of death.

So let's start again with a new ball – *the sun*
for pretending with balls is such fun.

There was a man

There was a man of whom t'was said
he lived too much inside his head,
so he decided one fine day
to send his head far, far away.

    He cupped his head in the palm of his hand
    as an athlete who puts the shot might do;
    then marked a distant point in the sand
    and, with a mighty heave, he threw
    (after whirling round three times or so)
    his head as far as it would go.
    For clarity it should be stated,
    (not as though you wouldn't know,
    given such a mighty throw),
    our friend was now decapitated.
    Head and body separated,
    body crumpled, slowly sinking;
    eyeballs twitched, then brain stopped thinking.
    Why should I, you may well wonder,
    tell you such a gory story,
    head and body split asunder,
    tragic act, bereft of glory?

This is why, I would suggest;
it is clearly for the best,
if you live inside your head,
better so, than to be dead.

And you who denigrate the mind,
who to the body feel inclined,
must here concede that bodies fade,
looks, limbs and muscle will degrade;
but thoughts, if great enough, will thrive
and will for centuries survive,
long after that which gave them birth
has turned to ashes, dust or earth.

Let critics carp, be not misled,
assert the truth, whatever's said.
If cynics sneer, this answer give:
"When all is said and done, the head
is not so bad a place to live";

And when the tyrant Time at last
arrives to extirpate your past,
assert this powerful paradigm –
the thought that thought can outwit time.

All you will need is to recall
a thought with power to enthral.
Should you need help, I would suggest,
the thought below will serve you best
and easily survive time's test.
Using a voice, both still and small,
these words will make time slow and stall:
"Love is the greatest thought of all."

The undoing of the rapper

I rap, my man,
because I can.
The words pour out
like water from
the perforated spout
of a watering can.
I have no plan.
Just want to shout.

Do not diss me.
When I'm a gonna
you will miss me.
You say I'm dense.
I don't make sense.
It's so bait; no debate.
I'm proud to be
inar_ticulate.

It ain't no crime
to stretch *a rhyme*
and stick it on
a line of song.
Don't get me wrong.
If I'm obscening without meaning,
who can tell?
So what the hell!

You don't get it?
Just forget it.
It's no prob;
it's not my job
to communicate –
for sure it ain't;
I just use words
like blobs of paint.

I don't mind.
I'm on grind.
So much skrilla,
it's a thriller.
Been playing hard
I'm going yard.
Need some nookie
and a cookie.

I'm no wasteman.
I make haste man
round my endz
in my Benz.
Be fair, you all,
be cool and civil;
don't you cavil
when I talk drivel.

Negation

I knew a man
who said he was,
but I replied,
a parting shot
that he was not.

I know a man
who likes to chant
"I am, I am,"
but I intone,
"You aren't."

"I will, I will,"
another cries.
but he will not
although I see
how hard he tries.

In dealing with such issues
– past, present, future state –
I always tend
to recommend
negate, negate, negate.

It's not that I'm averse to "Yes"
I see and feel its glow,
but when you dwell
in the mouth of hell
there's nothing quite like "No."

Whales never fail

Whales never fail
to give thanks
for the many banks
of plankton
and have no notion
of ill-doing
in their motion
though the ocean.

Polar bears
have no cares
in their slicing
through the ice;
they've no need to be sorry
for the feelings of their quarry
when the need to eat arises
and they make a seal a meal.

Just like imps,
little chimps,
when they can, like to rut,
if they're not engaged in grooming
or cracking the odd nut.

And the ruminating cow,
without complaint, accepts its fate
of endless chewing on the cud
in order to lactate.

The dog will lick his master's face,
present his wet and wayward nose,
the best friend man has ever had
and fearsome foe to all his foes.

But what a piece of work is man,
the wielder of the harshest rod,
who beats himself with demons
and an unforgiving god,
who elevates the psychopath
to leader of his clan,
a uniformed psychotic
with a death-delivering plan;
then honours such for raining death
upon his fellow man!

A parable of war

A flider on a goppel-gunge
was gloating on the floy,
when all at twice,
a guth of ice
beset a saneloi.

O flider on your gopple-gunge,
a-gloating on the floy,
while thus you lurk and somdel mote,
extatapath and iffidote,
a guth of ice with heffless joy,
is palming on a saneloi,
with cries of 'Frungen Frossinard,
EgaliPossiFraterard'.

"Alacaday O salitude!"
the flider then replied,
why do you trogate bluntedly
when it is plenimain to see
that he who neither guth may be,
nor, chance-a-joy, a saneloi,
must on a gopple-gunge reside.
A flider's role is sure to flide,
and this stoge gloi must all regard,
"Death or Frungen Frossinard,
EgaliPossiFraterard."

Ringwood wood

Should someone ask brave Robin Hood
to make a longbow if he could,
New Forest wood would be no good
but surely Ringwood Wood wood would.

Tricky

It's the same old story.
    In the fight for love and glory
    it has sadly gone all awry.
It's enough to make you cry.

An Amorusc expedition

A mollusc and an egg set out
for the land where love is made.
The mollusc pulled a mussel
while the egg itself got laid.

Evolution

If evolution prompts hysteria
or makes us think we are superia
then here's a thought that's even queeria –
a cursory glance at our interia
suggests that we are really hereia
as perfect fodder for bacteria,
a role demeaning and inferia.

Oh Dearia!

Index of First Lines

A flider on a gopple-gunge	183
A man, in every circumstance	101
A man within four walls confined	117
A mollusc and an egg set out	181
Anger	94
A physicist pig	169
At the end of yesterday	29
Banished was I from the heart of Arabia	149
Bones, beneath the skin of metaphor	68
Dry leaves, wizened, lifeless	115
Even a busy urban man may find	106
Faim for le fromage	170
For me you weave a mystery	4
How many times have you and I	14
I am the creator	121
I am, therefore I am	123
I am weary	49
I knew a man	176
I know God, a dirty old man	61
I rap, my man	174
I saw you born. You came into this world	144
I sleep, I cease to be	113
I was seated one day	31
I would that God would stand and spare	88
I'm a pongpoidal person	165
I'm afraid	36
I'm losing myself within my head	37
If evolution prompts hysteria	181
If I had been	110
If I to you	7
If I was God and I was bored	70
In a land long ago	161

In the beginning	3
In the silent times of dreaming	54
It is possible	62
It starts, a cold, blank, empty stare	126
It's obvious to anyone who thinks	130
It's the same old story	180
Let's agree that	84
Let's pretend	171
Lethargic lions lurk along our motorways	57
Listen to me, lovely, lissom-limbed daughter of Zeus	22
"Love," and she clung to me	38
Love distilled	98
Love is made	35
Never a word so much abused as love	10
Not moist, red lips, nor limpid eyes	9
O Lord, we, the management	64
Oh! Pongipoid!	166
On a bright summer's day, when the sun was a-roastin	152
One should never leave one's home	102
Our Father	72
Our love, my love	21
Poor old dear	33
Potatoes, peas, pornography	27
Should someone ask brave Robin Hood	180
So that's the way it is, my God, no chance	41
So there you are, my god, my god	76
Stand on the castle parapet with me	45
Take time with me to ponder this	81
Tell me a story of ancient times	15
That man who limps	108
That out of nothing something comes	73
The bride requested I take time	139
The elephant's skin	167
The game is done, the die is cast	134
The hunter's moon is high tonight	53

The knife, high-poised above the stone	56
The open road	93
The twig that falls	112
The wind wanders by, through the streets of the town	160
There is a world the depth of which I am afraid	58
There is no way of telling when	19
There was a man of whom t'was said	172
There's a way you can pray	159
They lied beyond all limit when	107
They passed the day	17
This then I swear	91
Time drift	5
Today I'm going to share with you	131
Too many choices	40
Two thousand weeks hence	12
Venus arose, while Mars was yet abed	105
We hear the children laughing	96
We see effects and think we know	128
Whales never fail	177
When I was young	118
When people babble through the day	104
Who told the child that cried	114
Why should the God who made the world	79
You are as empty as the sea	39

www.ingramcontent.com/pod-product-compliance
Lightning Source LLC
Chambersburg PA
CBHW070553010526
44118CB00012B/1307